POC

Operational Management

Level 5

MCI, Russell Square House, 10-12 Russell Square, London WC1B 5BZ
Telephone 0171 872 9000
Website http://www.bbi.co.uk/mci
e-mail nfmed_mci@compuserve.com
Registered Charity No. 1002554

Management Charter Initiative is the operating arm of the National
Forum for Management Education and Development.

The National Occupational Standard for Management was developed by MCI with funding from
the Department for Education and Employment.

First published 1998

ISBN 1 897587 77 5

Text processing and typesetting by Digital Type
Printed and bound in Great Britain by Cambridge University Press

Contents

Introduction   1

Management Standards

  Mandatory Units

    Unit A3   Manage activities to meet customer requirements   6

    Unit A5   Manage change in organisational activities   16

    Unit B4   Determine the effective use of resources   28

    Unit C3   Enhance your own performance   36

    Unit C6   Enhance productive working relationships   42

    Unit D6   Use information to take critical decisions   50

  Optional Units

    Unit B5   Secure financial resources for your organisation's plans   62

    Unit C8   Select personnel for activities   70

    Unit C10 Develop teams and individuals to enhance performance   76

    Unit C13 Manage the performance of teams and individuals   90

    Unit C16 Deal with poor performance in your team   100

    Unit C17 Redeploy personnel and make redundancies   108

    Unit D3   Chair and participate in meetings   116

    Unit D5   Establish information management and communication systems   122

    Unit E1   Identify the scope for improvement in the way the organisation manages energy   132

    Unit E3   Promote energy efficiency   138

    Unit F1   Promote the importance and benefits of quality   144

    Unit F3   Manage continuous quality improvement   150

    Unit F4   Implement quality assurance systems   156

    Unit F6   Monitor compliance with quality systems   164

    Unit G4   Plan and prepare projects   172

    Unit G5   Manage the running of projects   180

    Unit G6   Complete projects   190

Index   197

Acknowledgements

MCI gratefully acknowledges the assistance of over 4,000 managers and hundreds of employing organisations from all sectors of the economy who participated in the revision and piloting of these standards; the financial support of the Department for Education and Employment; and the Steering Group members, individuals, consultants and MCI staff who have contributed to the development and authorship of this publication.

Management Standards and Qualifications

Developed through consultation with tens of thousands of managers throughout the private, public and voluntary sectors, the Management Standards define benchmarks of best practice in management in the UK today. They describe the standard of performance which is expected of you in the wide variety of functions you carry out as a manager.

If you can prove to an assessor that you consistently perform to these *National Standards*, you can be awarded a National Vocational Qualification (NVQ) or Scottish Vocational Qualification (SVQ). NVQs and SVQs in Management are available at the three highest levels, known as levels 3, 4 and 5 (levels 1 and 2 cover technical, administrative and other non-management functions).

This booklet *Operational Management Level 5* covers all the units of the Management Standards for NVQ/SVQ level 5 in Operational Management. It is for you if you are a practising manager and:

- have operational responsibility for substantial programmes and resources
- have a broad span of control
- proactively identify and implement change and quality improvements
- negotiate budgets and contracts, *and*
- lead high level meetings.

If you are aspiring to become a senior operational manager, you will find these standards a useful guide to what will be expected of you as a manager working at this level.

Units of Competence

The Management Standards are expressed in a number of *units of competence*, each unit describing a specific management function. The units contain *performance criteria*, clear statements which allow you to assess whether you are performing to the national standard. If you are taking an NVQ or SVQ, your assessor will need to be sure you consistently meet all these criteria in order to certify that you are competent.

The standards specify *knowledge requirements*, what you need to know and understand in order to perform to the national standard. They also identify the *personal competencies*, the skills and attitudes which are essential for effective performance, described as behaviours which it is possible to observe. You can therefore read appropriate management books or attend development programmes to ensure you have the necessary knowledge and skills. If you are unsure about your performance in a particular area, you can use the Management Standards to diagnose the knowledge or skills development you require.

Finally, the standards specify *evidence requirements*. These clearly state the evidence you need to convince your NVQ/SVQ assessor or your line manager that you are competent.

Coverage of Operational Management Level 5

Operational Management Level 5 covers the full range of general management activities which managers working at this level are expected to carry out. It does not, however, cover specialist functions (such as sales, accounting or engineering) which are covered by other, specialist standards.

You will find your work as a manager is reflected in the four generic key roles: *A Manage Activities, B Manage Resources, C*

Management Standards and Qualifications

Manage People and *D Manage Information*. You may also have some specialist responsibilities which are covered in the specialist management key roles of *E Manage Energy*, *F Manage Quality* and *G Manage Projects*.

Unit A3 *Manage activities to meet customer requirements* involves agreeing requirements with your customers, planning work activities and monitoring these activities to ensure that your customers' requirements have been met.

Unit A5 *Manage change in organisational activities* covers identifying possible areas for improvement, considering the feasibility of proposed changes, planning the implementation of change, reaching agreement with those involved and finally implementing the planned changes.

Unit B4 *Determine the effective use of resources* covers making proposals for expenditure, agreeing budgets and controlling activities so that they operate within budget.

Unit B5 *Secure financial resources for your organisation's plans* covers examining the way your organisation generates and allocates financial resources, evaluating proposals from others on expenditure, and obtaining the financial resources which your organisation needs.

Unit C3 *Enhance your own performance* is about continuously developing your knowledge and skills and optimising your use of your time and resources to meet your objectives.

Unit C6 *Enhance productive working relationships* is about enhancing relationships with colleagues in your organisation. It also involves providing guidance on your organisation's values and how to work in accordance with these values.

Unit C8 *Select personnel for activities* is about recruiting and selecting the people you need to carry out your work activities.

Unit C10 *Develop teams and individuals to enhance performance* covers identifying people's development needs, planning their development and using a variety of means to improve team performance.

Unit C13 *Manage the performance of teams and individuals* covers allocating work, agreeing objectives, setting out plans and methods of working, monitoring and evaluating work and providing feedback to people on their performance.

Unit C16 *Deal with poor performance* in your team is about dealing with team members whose performance is unsatisfactory. It covers providing support, contributing to disciplinary and grievance procedures and dismissing team members if no other course is possible.

Unit C17 *Redeploy personnel and make redundancies* is about transferring people to other posts and making staff redundant in response to developments and structural change.

Unit D3 *Chair and participate in meetings* is about leading and contributing to meetings to achieve objectives.

Unit D5 *Establish information management and communication systems* covers identifying, selecting, setting up and monitoring systems in your organisation.

Unit D6 *Use information to take critical decisions* covers obtaining and analysing information to take decisions and advising and informing other people.

The 'E' units, 'F' units and 'G' units are specialist units and cover managing energy, quality and projects respectively.

Gaining a Management NVQ or SVQ

To be assessed for a Management NVQ or SVQ, you must register with an approved centre (details available from MCI). In contrast to academic qualifications, with NVQs and SVQs there is no prescribed course of study. The centre will provide you with advice on any areas where you need to develop new knowledge and skills. The centre itself may offer management development programmes, or it may refer you to other management courses, text books, open and flexible learning schemes or other development activities.

The centre will also provide you with guidance on how to prepare for assessment and allocate you an assessor who will assess your competence. If you are taking and NVQ/SVQ in Operational Management Level 5, you will be assessed against the 6 mandatory units (highlighted in bold in the previous section), plus any four other units which you are free to choose.

You will need to gather evidence of your competence which will include products and outcomes of your work activities as well as short reports of your own and statements from others who have observed your performance. You will submit this evidence to your assessor together with your claim for competence. After an assessment interview, your assessor will make one of

three credit recommendations: that you are competent, not yet competent, or that you have not provided sufficient evidence to make a decision. If you are assessed as competent, you will be awarded your NVQ or SVQ.

Operational Management

Level 5

NVQ/SVQ

Mandatory units
Candidates take ALL 6 mandatory units

Manage activities to meet customer requirements

Unit summary

This unit is about managing activities and conditions in the workplace to meet your customers' requirements. This involves agreeing requirements with your customers, planning work activities and monitoring these activities to ensure that your customers' requirements have been met. It also involves maintaining a suitable work environment and continuously looking for ways to improve working conditions and processes.

This unit contains four elements

A3.1 *Agree customer requirements;*
A3.2 *Plan activities to meet customer requirements;*
A3.3 *Maintain a healthy, safe and productive work environment;*
A3.4 *Ensure products and services meet customer requirements.*

Personal competencies

In performing effectively in this unit, you will show that you

Building teams
- keep others informed about plans and progress
- clearly identify what is required of others
- invite others to contribute to planning and organising work

Communicating
- identify the information needs of listeners
- adopt communication styles appropriate to listeners and situations, including selecting an appropriate time and place
- present difficult ideas and problems in ways that promote understanding
- encourage listeners to ask questions or rephrase statements to clarify their understanding

Focusing on results
- maintain a focus on objectives
- tackle problems and take advantage of opportunities as they arise
- actively seek to do things better
- use change as an opportunity for improvement
- monitor quality of work and progress against plans

Influencing others
- present yourself positively to others
- create and prepare strategies for influencing others
- use a variety of means to influence others

Thinking and taking decisions
- break processes down into tasks and activities
- identify a range of elements in and perspectives on a situation
- identify implications, consequences or causal relationships in a situation
- take decisions which are realistic for the situation.

Manage activities to meet customer requirements

Element A3.1

Agree customer requirements

Performance criteria

You must ensure that

a) you give **customers** opportunities to specify their requirements

b) you give **customers** clear and accurate information regarding the features and benefits of products and services

c) the agreements you make with **customers** contain all relevant information to specify the work activities necessary to meet their requirements

d) the agreements you make with **customers** meet legal and **organisational requirements**

e) you record, store and use information provided by **customers** in ways which are consistent with legal and **organisational requirements**

f) you regularly review **customer** agreements and the process of reaching these agreements in order to identify improvements which can be made.

Knowledge requirements

You need to know and understand

Agreements and contracts
- different forms of agreements which may be used and their relative advantages and disadvantages to your area of work
- organisational and legal requirements regarding contracts and other forms of agreement and their implications for your work
- how to record agreements and what information these agreements should contain

Communication
- the principles and processes of effective communication and how to apply them

Continuous improvement
- the importance of regularly reviewing customer agreements and the processes used and how to do so

Customer relations
- the importance of a focus on customer requirements and quality issues, and your role and responsibilities in relation to this
- how to negotiate with and influence potential and actual customers
- the difference between internal and external customers
- how to reach agreements with customers on their needs and requirements

Information handling
- the principles of confidentiality: types of information which should be regarded as confidential and how this information should be handled

Organisational context
- product information relevant to your area of responsibility
- the standards and organisational policies relevant to your area of responsibility.

Evidence requirements

You must prove that you *agree customer requirements* to the National Standard of competence.

To do this, you must provide evidence to convince your assessor that you consistently meet **all** the performance criteria.

Your evidence must be the result of real work activities undertaken by yourself. Evidence from simulated activities is **not** acceptable for this element.

You must show evidence that you agree requirements with **one** of the following types of **customer**
- internal
- external.

You must also show evidence that your agreements meet **all** the following types of **organisational requirements**
- quality standards
- organisational policies
- organisational objectives.

You must, however, convince your assessor that you have the necessary knowledge, understanding and skills to be able to perform competently in respect of **all** types of **customers,** listed above.

Manage activities to meet customer requirements

Element A3.2

Plan activities to meet customer requirements

Performance criteria

You must ensure that

a) you give opportunities to **relevant people** to help **plan** activities to meet customer requirements

b) your **plans** take into account your experience of past activities, the current availability of resources and likely future circumstances which may affect your **plans**

c) your **plans** allow customer requirements to be met within the agreed time scales

d) your **plans** are consistent with your organisation's objectives and policies, and with relevant legal requirements

e) you present your **plans** to **relevant people** in an appropriate and timely manner

f) you confirm people's understanding of, and commitment to, **plans** at appropriate intervals.

Knowledge requirements

You need to know and understand

Communication
- how to organise, present and communicate plans effectively according to the needs of different people within the organisation

Continuous improvement
- the results of evaluations of previous relevant plans and activities and how to use these results to improve present practice

Involvement and motivation
- the importance of encouraging people to contribute to the planning process; what contributions these people may make to the planning process, and how to encourage their collaboration

Organisational context
- the organisational objectives, policies and legal requirements which are relevant to your responsibilities for planning and the implications for your work

Planning
- the importance of effective planning in the management of activities to meet customer requirements and your role and responsibility in relation to this
- the principles of planning activities so that customer requirements can be met
- the principles of effective time and resource management.

Evidence requirements

You must prove that you *plan activities to meet customer requirements* to the National Standard of competence.

To do this, you must provide evidence to convince your assessor that you consistently meet **all** the performance criteria.

Your evidence must be the result of real work activities undertaken by yourself. Evidence from simulated activities is **not** acceptable for this element.

You must show that you provide opportunities for making recommendations and present plans to **two** of the following types of **relevant people**
- team members
- colleagues working at your level
- higher-level managers or sponsors
- people outside your organisation.

You must also show evidence of producing **two plans**, one of which must be in written form (or in another suitable permanent format, if you have a visual impairment).

You must, however, convince your assessor that you have the necessary knowledge, understanding and skills to be able to perform competently in respect of **all** types of **relevant people,** listed above.

**Manage activities to meet
customer requirements**

Element A3.3

Maintain a healthy, safe and productive work environment

Performance criteria

You must ensure that

a) you inform **relevant people** about their legal and organisational responsibilities for maintaining a healthy, safe and productive **work environment**

b) you make sufficient support available to **relevant people** to ensure they can work in a healthy, safe and productive way

c) you provide opportunities for **relevant people** to make recommendations for improving the **work environment**

d) the **work environment** within your control conforms to organisational and legal requirements

e) the **work environment** is as conducive to productive work activity as possible within organisational constraints

f) you deal with breaches in health and safety requirements promptly and in line with organisational and legal requirements

g) you make recommendations for improving the **work environment** clearly and promptly to **relevant people**

h) your records concerning health and safety and the **work environment** are complete, accurate and comply with organisational and legal requirements.

Knowledge requirements

You need to know and understand

Analytical techniques
- the principles of risk assessment and how to ensure that the work environment is effectively monitored
- methods of assessing current working conditions and identifying possible areas for improvement

Communication
- how to communicate effectively with team members, colleagues, line managers and people outside your organisation

Health and safety
- the importance of health and safety at work and your role and responsibility in relation to this
- the organisational and legal requirements for maintaining a healthy, safe and productive work environment
- industry or profession specific codes of practice relevant to healthy, safe and productive work environments
- the types of support it may be necessary to provide on health and safety issues and how to provide such support
- how to respond to contradictions between health and safety requirements and organisational constraints

Organisational context
- the procedures to follow in order to recommend improvements in the work environment
- the records which you need to keep and the organisational and legislative requirements for doing so

Workplace organisation
- the types of work environments which are most conducive to productive work.

Evidence requirements

You must prove that you *maintain a healthy, safe and productive work environment* to the National Standard of competence.

To do this, you must provide evidence to convince your assessor that you consistently meet **all** the performance criteria.

Your evidence must be the result of real work activities undertaken by yourself. Evidence from simulated activities is acceptable **only** for performance criterion f) in this element.

You must show evidence that you provide information, support and recommendations to **two** of the following types of **relevant people**
- team members
- colleagues working at your level
- higher-level managers or sponsors
- people outside your organisation.

Your evidence must cover **all** the following features of the **work environment**
- physical environment
- equipment
- materials
- working procedures.

You must, however, convince your assessor that you have the necessary knowledge, understanding and skills to be able to perform competently in respect of **all** types of **relevant people,** listed above.

Manage activities to meet
customer requirements

Element A3.4

Ensure products and services meet customer requirements

Performance criteria

You must ensure that

a) you give opportunities to **relevant people** to monitor the quality of products and services and recommend improvements to the processes involved

b) your monitoring of the quality of products and services is continuous and complies with organisational procedures

c) you give support to **relevant people** so they can maintain and improve quality

d) you give opportunities to your customers to provide feedback on how effectively their requirements are being met

e) you communicate with customers clearly, accurately and promptly when there are significant changes to products and services

f) the products and services within your area of responsibility normally meet your customers' and **organisation's requirements**

g) where products, services and the processes involved do not meet agreed requirements, you take prompt and effective action

h) your records relating to customer service and quality comply with organisational procedures.

Knowledge requirements

You need to know and understand

Communication

- the principles and processes of effective communication and how to apply them

Customer relations

- the importance of customer feedback and how to encourage it
- how to communicate effectively with customers

Monitoring and evaluation

- how to monitor the quality of work taking place in your area of responsibility

Organisational context

- the standards, customer and organisational requirements which apply to the activities for which you are responsible
- how to interpret organisational values and policies and determine the implications for quality assurance
- the records which need to be completed and how this should be done

Quality management

- the meaning and importance of quality in the management of activities and your role and responsibilities in relation to this
- the principles and methods of quality assurance
- the importance of encouraging team members and others to monitor quality processes and recommend improvements to practice
- deficiencies in quality that are likely to occur and the appropriate corrective actions to take, whilst minimising the impact on customers.

Evidence requirements

You must prove that you *ensure products and services meet customer requirements* to the National Standard of competence.

To do this, you must provide evidence to convince your assessor that you consistently meet **all** the performance criteria.

Your evidence must be the result of real work activities undertaken by yourself. Evidence from simulated activities is **not** acceptable for this element.

You must show evidence that you provide opportunities for suggestions and make recommendations to **two** of the following types of **relevant people**
- team members
- colleagues working at the same level
- higher-level managers or sponsors
- specialists.

You must also show evidence that you meet **all** the following types of **organisational requirements**
- quality standards
- organisational policies
- organisational objectives.

You must, however, convince your assessor that you have the necessary knowledge, understanding and skills to be able to perform competently in respect of **all** types of **relevant people,** listed above.

Manage change in organisational activities

Unit summary

This unit is about improving the operational activities under your control and managing the necessary changes effectively. It covers identifying possible areas for improvement, considering the feasibility of proposed changes, planning the implementation of change, reaching agreement with those involved and finally implementing the planned changes.

The unit contains five elements

A5.1   *Identify opportunities for improvements in activities*
A5.2   *Evaluate proposed changes for benefits and disadvantages*
A5.3   *Plan the implementation of change in activities*
A5.4   *Agree the introduction of change*
A5.5   *Implement changes in activities.*

Personal competencies

In performing effectively in this unit, you will show that you

Communicating
- identify the information needs of listeners
- adopt communication styles appropriate to listeners and situations, including selecting an appropriate time and place
- use a variety of media and communication aids to reinforce points and maintain interest
- encourage listeners to ask questions or rephrase statements to clarify their understanding

Focusing on results
- tackle problems and take advantage of opportunities as they arise
- prioritise objectives and schedule work to make best use of time and resources
- focus personal attention on specific details that are critical to the success of a key event
- use change as an opportunity for improvement
- monitor quality of work and progress against plans

Influencing others
- present yourself positively to others
- create and prepare strategies for influencing others
- use a variety of means to influence others
- understand the culture of the organisation and act to work within it or influence it

Searching for information
- seek information from multiple sources
- challenge the validity and reliability of sources of information

Thinking and taking decisions
- break processes down into tasks and activities
- identify implications, consequences or causal relationships in a situation
- use your own experience and evidence from others to identify problems and understand situations
- produce a variety of solutions before taking a decision
- take decisions which are realistic for the situation.

Manage change in
organisational activities

Element A5.1

Identify opportunities for improvements in activities

Performance criteria

You must ensure that

a) you **monitor** and evaluate activities at intervals most likely to reveal potential improvements

b) the information you gather on trends and developments is relevant, valid, reliable and sufficient to identify potential improvements

c) you give opportunities to **relevant people** to make recommendations for improvements in activities

d) the improvements you identify are realistic and consistent with your organisation's values and objectives

e) you provide clear and accurate information regarding identified improvements to **relevant people** at an appropriate time.

Knowledge requirements

You need to know and understand

Analytical techniques
- how to assess recommendations to check whether they are realistic

Communication
- how to communicate effectively with your team members, colleagues, line managers and specialists

Continuous improvement
- the importance of the continuous improvement in activities to the effectiveness of the organisation and your role and responsibilities in relation to this

Information handling
- the types of information on internal and external trends needed to identify potential improvements and how to validate such information

Involvement and motivation
- the importance of empowering other staff to make recommendations to improve work activities and how to encourage them to do so

Monitoring and evaluation
- how to monitor and assess the effectiveness and efficiency of activities and identify potential improvements

Organisational context
- the structure of your organisation and the responsibilities of people within it
- the organisational values and objectives which have a bearing on the recommendations you are making and how to interpret their implications.

Evidence requirements

You must prove that you *identify opportunities for improvements in activities* to the National Standard of competence.

To do this, you must provide evidence to convince your assessor that you consistently meet **all** the performance criteria.

Your evidence must be the result of real work activities undertaken by yourself. Evidence from simulated activities is **not** acceptable for this element.

You must show evidence that you use at least **two** of the following types of **monitoring** methods
- direct observation
- considering oral information from others
- examining written information from others.

You must show evidence that you provide information on identified improvements to at least **two** of the following types of **relevant people**
- team members
- colleagues working at the same level
- higher-level managers or sponsors
- specialists.

You must, however, convince your assessor that you have the necessary knowledge, understanding and skills to be able to perform competently in respect of **all** types of **monitoring** and **relevant people,** listed above.

Manage change in organisational activities

Evaluate proposed changes for benefits and disadvantages

Performance criteria

You must ensure that

a) you get complete and accurate information to evaluate current and proposed products and services and the processes involved

b) you evaluate current and proposed products, services and processes accurately, and identify their relative benefits and disadvantages

c) your **analysis** of the implications of proposed changes is accurate and comprehensive

d) you provide opportunities for **relevant people** to help evaluate proposed changes

e) your evaluation of proposed changes takes account of previous experience and likely future circumstances

f) your final recommendations integrate contributions from **relevant people**, where appropriate.

Knowledge requirements

You need to know and understand

Analytical techniques
- how to evaluate proposed changes for benefits and disadvantages
- how to analyse the required information, both qualitatively and quantitatively

Communication
- the principles and processes of effective communication and how to apply them

Information handling
- the types of information you need to evaluate proposed changes and how to validate such information

Involvement and motivation
- the importance of encouraging others to contribute to the evaluation of proposed changes and how to do so
- the importance of integrating all appropriate views and opinions into the final recommendations

Organisational context
- the structure of your organisation and the responsibilities of people within it

Planning
- the previous experience of change relevant to the current proposals and its implication for what you are proposing.

Evidence requirements

You must prove that you *evaluate proposed changes for benefits and disadvantages* to the National Standard of competence.

To do this, you must provide evidence to convince your assessor that you consistently meet **all** the performance criteria.

Your evidence must be the result of real work activities undertaken by yourself. Evidence from simulated activities is **not** acceptable for this element.

You must show evidence that you use **both** of the following types of **analysis**
- qualitative
- quantitative.

You must show evidence that you can involve at least **three** of the following types of **relevant people**
- team members
- colleagues working at the same level as yourself
- higher-level managers or sponsors
- people outside your organisation
- specialists.

You must, however, convince your assessor that you have the necessary knowledge, understanding and skills to be able to perform competently in respect of **all** types of **relevant people**, listed above.

Manage change in organisational activities

Element A5.3

Plan the implementation of change in activities

Performance criteria

You must ensure that

a) you provide clear and accurate information on the proposed change to **relevant people** at appropriate times

b) you give opportunities for **relevant people** to comment on the proposed change and contribute to planning its implementation

c) the way you identify and evaluate **obstacles** to change enables you to overcome them effectively

d) your plans for the implementation of change are detailed, comprehensive, accurate and consistent with organisational objectives

e) you make a clear case for the proposed change and support your case with sound evidence

f) your implementation plans integrate contributions from **relevant people**, where appropriate

g) your plans clearly identify the implications for, and the roles of, all those involved in the proposed change.

Knowledge requirements

You need to know and understand

Analytical techniques
- how to identify and evaluate potential obstacles to change and produce solutions which minimise their impact on what is proposed

Change management
- the principles underpinning the management of change
- how to make and argue an effective case for change

Communication
- the principles and processes of effective communication and how to apply them
- the principles of consultation and negotiation in the management of change and how to apply them

Involvement and motivation
- how to gain the commitment of people to the change process

Organisational context
- the structure of your organisation and the responsibilities of people within it

Planning
- the importance of planning for the management of change and how such plans should be made.

Evidence requirements

You must prove that you *plan the implementation of change in activities* to the National Standard of competence.

To do this, you must provide evidence to convince your assessor that you consistently meet **all** the performance criteria.

Your evidence must be the result of real work activities undertaken by yourself. Evidence from simulated activities is **not** acceptable for this element.

You must show evidence that you can involve at least **three** of the following types of **relevant people**
- team members
- colleagues working at the same level as yourself
- higher-level managers or sponsors
- people outside the organisation
- specialists.

You must show evidence that you identify and evaluate at least **one** of the following types of **obstacles**
- internal
- external.

You must, however, convince your assessor that you have the necessary knowledge, understanding and skills to be able to perform competently in respect of **all** types of **relevant people** and **obstacles,** listed above.

Manage change in organisational activities

Element A5.4

Agree the introduction of change

Performance criteria

You must ensure that

a) you present plans for the introduction of change clearly

b) you identify the nature and benefits of the change and the implications for all **relevant people**

c) you check and confirm **relevant people's** understanding of the implications of the change and their commitment to their role in the process

d) any compromises you make during **negotiations** on the implementation of change result in modifications to plans which are consistent with the objectives of the change

e) you conduct **negotiations** in a manner which maintains good working relationships with those involved

f) you present any reasons for not reaching agreement on the introduction of change to **relevant people** in a manner which maintains morale and motivation.

Knowledge requirements

You need to know and understand

Change management

- how to identify and evaluate the implications of proposed changes for people in the organisation
- how to make and argue an effective case for change
- the importance of negotiation and consultation in the management of change and methods to do so
- how to respond when agreement on change cannot be reached

Communication

- the principles and processes of effective communication and how to apply them
- the importance of clear communication in the management of change and the types of information which need to be communicated to different groups of people

Organisational context

- the structure of your organisation and the responsibilities of people within it.

Evidence requirements

You must prove that you *agree the introduction of change* to the National Standard of competence.

To do this, you must provide evidence to convince your assessor that you consistently meet **all** the performance criteria.

Your evidence must be the result of real work activities undertaken by yourself. Evidence from simulated activities is **not** acceptable for this element.

You must show evidence that you can involve at least **three** of the following types of **relevant people**

- team members
- colleagues working at the same level as yourself
- higher-level managers or sponsors
- people outside the organisation
- specialists.

You must show evidence that you carry out at least **one** of the following types of **negotiations**

- spoken
- written.

You must, however, convince your assessor that you have the necessary knowledge, understanding and skills to be able to perform competently in respect of **all** types of **relevant people** and **negotiations**, listed above.

**Manage change in
organisational activities**

Element A5.5

Implement changes in activities

Performance criteria

You must ensure that

a) you present your plans for implementing changes at a time, level and pace appropriate for those involved

b) the resources and support you provide to those involved are sufficient for the changes to take place within agreed time scales

c) your **monitoring** and **evaluation** of the changes takes place at appropriate times against agreed implementation plans

d) the modifications you make to implementation activities are sufficient to resolve any problems arising

e) the way in which you implement changes enables **relevant people** to contribute to the process effectively

f) you achieve the results you anticipate from the changes within agreed time scales

g) you maintain the quality of work to an agreed standard throughout the period of change

h) your **monitoring** and **evaluation** records are clear, accurate and available only to authorised people.

Knowledge requirements

You need to know and understand

Change management
- how to identify the implications of change for the quality of the organisation's work and strategies to minimise adverse effects

Communication
- the principles and processes of effective communication and how to apply them
- the importance of clear communication in the management of change and what types of information need to be communicated to which groups of people

Involvement and motivation
- the importance of enabling those affected by change to contribute to the style of implementation and how to achieve this

Monitoring and evaluation
- the importance of monitoring and evaluating change and how to do so

Organisational context
- the structure of your organisation and the responsibilities of people within it

Planning
- how to develop an effective action plan for change.

Evidence requirements

You must prove that you *implement changes in activities* to the National Standard of competence.

To do this, you must provide evidence to convince your assessor that you consistently meet **all** the performance criteria.

Your evidence must be the result of real work activities undertaken by yourself. Evidence from simulated activities is **not** acceptable for this element.

You must show evidence that you use at least **two** of the following types of **monitoring** methods
- direct observation
- considering oral information
- examining written information.

You must show evidence that you use **both** of the following types of **evaluation**
- quantitative
- qualitative.

You must also show evidence that you can involve at least **three** of the following types of **relevant people**
- team members
- colleagues working at the same level as yourself
- higher-level managers or sponsors
- people outside the organisation
- specialists.

You must, however, convince your assessor that you have the necessary knowledge, understanding and skills to be able to perform competently in respect of **all** types of **monitoring** and **relevant people**, listed above.

Determine the effective use of resources

Unit summary

This unit is about the efficient management of resources across substantial programmes of work. It covers making proposals for expenditure, agreeing budgets and controlling activities so that they operate within budget.

This unit contains three elements

B4.1 *Make proposals for expenditure on programmes of work*
B4.2 *Agree budgets for programmes of work*
B4.3 *Control expenditure and activities against budgets.*

Personal competencies

In performing effectively in this unit, you will show that you

Communicating
- listen actively, ask questions, clarify points and rephrase others' statements to check mutual understanding
- identify the information needs of listeners
- adopt communication styles appropriate to listeners and situations, including selecting an appropriate time and place

Focusing on results
- maintain a focus on objectives
- tackle problems and take advantage of opportunities as they arise
- prioritise objectives and schedule work to make best use of time and resources
- focus personal attention on specific details that are critical to the success of a key event
- monitor quality of work and progress against plans

Influencing others
- develop and use contacts to trade information, and obtain support and resources
- present yourself positively to others
- create and prepare strategies for influencing others
- use a variety of means to influence others
- understand the culture of your organisation and act to work within it or influence it

Searching for information
- seek information from multiple sources
- challenge the validity and reliability of sources of information

Thinking and taking decisions
- break processes down into tasks and activities
- identify a range of elements in and perspectives on a situation
- identify implications, consequences or causal relationships in a situation
- use your own experience and evidence from others to identify problems and understand situations
- produce a variety of solutions before taking a decision
- take decisions which are realistic for the situation.

Determine the effective use of
resources

Element B4.1

Make proposals for expenditure on programmes of work

Performance criteria

You must ensure that

a) you give opportunities to **relevant people** to help develop your **proposals** for **expenditure**

b) your **proposals** take account of past **expenditure**

c) your **proposals** take account of trends, developments and other factors likely to affect future **expenditure**

d) your **proposals** clearly show how the programme contributes to organisational objectives and strategies

e) your **proposals** include targets, standards and monitoring methods

f) your **proposals** contain a financial justification and sufficient, valid information to allow your **proposals** to be evaluated realistically

g) you present your **proposals** to **relevant people** in an appropriate format and at an appropriate time.

Knowledge requirements

You need to know and understand

Analytical techniques
- how to analyse expenditure on programmes of work in the past and use the results to improve future use
- how to carry out cost-benefit analyses in regard to expenditure
- how to decide on targets, standards and monitoring methods

Communication
- how to develop and argue an effective case for expenditure

Information handling
- the kinds of trends and developments which might influence future expenditure
- how to collect and validate information required to evaluate a case for expenditure
- the types of information required to make decisions on expenditure

Involvement and motivation
- how to enable people to contribute to proposals

Organisational context
- the organisational objectives and strategies relevant to the programmes of work
- the procedures which need to be followed to make expenditure proposals

Resource management
- the importance of expenditure planning to organisational efficiency and your role and responsibility in relation to this
- the principles which underpin effective expenditure planning.

Evidence requirements

You must prove that you *make proposals for expenditure on programmes of work* to the National Standard of competence.

To do this, you must provide evidence to convince your assessor that you consistently meet **all** the performance criteria.

Your evidence must be the result of real work activities undertaken by yourself. Evidence from simulated activities is **not** acceptable for this element.

You must show evidence that you seek contributions from **two** of the following types of **relevant people**
- team members
- colleagues working at the same level
- higher-level managers or sponsors
- financial specialists
- people outside your organisation.

You must show evidence that your proposals cover **expenditure** on **two** of the following types of items
- supplies of goods
- supplies of services
- people
- overhead expenses
- capital equipment
- premises.

You must also show evidence that you make **both** of the following types of **proposals**
- medium term
- long term.

You must, however, convince your assessor that you have the necessary knowledge, understanding and skills to be able to perform competently in respect of **all** types of **relevant people** and **expenditure**, listed above.

Determine the effective use of
resources

Element B4.2

Agree budgets for programmes of work

Performance criteria

You must ensure that

a) you give opportunities to **relevant people** to participate in negotiating and agreeing **budgets** for programmes of work

b) your **budget** proposals are clear, concise and emphasise the benefits to your organisation

c) you present **budget** proposals in a way which reflects the commitment of those who will be responsible for the programmes of work

d) your **budget** proposals are based on an accurate interpretation of valid data and a realistic evaluation of risk

e) you clarify and resolve any areas of uncertainty and disagreement over the proposed **budget**

f) you negotiate **budgets** in a way which maintains good relationships with the people involved

g) you complete your **budget** negotiations within agreed time scales

h) you provide **relevant people** with accurate information on **budget** decisions in a manner and at a time which is likely to ensure their co-operation and confidence.

Knowledge requirements

You need to know and understand

Analytical techniques
- how to analyse the possible risks to the organisation associated with proposed budgets

Budgets
- the importance of clear and accurate budgets to the running of programmes of work and your role and responsibility in relation to this
- the principles of budgeting and how to apply them
- the importance of gaining agreement to budgets and how to carry out budget negotiations
- areas of uncertainty and disagreement which may occur when agreeing budgets and how to resolve these in a way which is satisfactory to those involved in the decision-making process

Communication
- how to present budgets in a way which is likely to gain the support of key decision makers
- how to communicate budget information effectively to relevant people

Information handling
- the types of information required to develop budgets and how to validate these

Involvement and motivation
- how to encourage and enable people to take part in the negotiation and agreement of budgets for programmes of work
- how to gain the commitment of team members to proposed budgets.

Evidence requirements

You must prove that you *agree budgets for programmes of work* to the National Standard of competence.

To do this, you must provide evidence to convince your assessor that you consistently meet **all** the performance criteria.

Your evidence must be the result of real work activities undertaken by yourself. Evidence from simulated activities is **not** acceptable for this element.

You must show evidence that you agree **both** of the following types of **budgets**
- for programmes of work within your area of responsibility
- for sharing of overhead charges with others.

You must show evidence that you can involve **two** of the following types of **relevant people** in negotiations and provide them with information on budget decisions
- team members
- colleagues working at the same level as yourself
- higher-level managers or sponsors
- financial specialists
- people outside your organisation.

You must, however, convince your assessor that you have the necessary knowledge, understanding and skills to be able to perform competently in respect of **all** types of **relevant people**, listed above.

Determine the effective use of resources

Element B4.3

Control expenditure and activities against budgets

Performance criteria

You must ensure that

a) you give opportunities to team members to take individual responsibility for **monitoring** and controlling **expenditure** and activities against **budgets**

b) your methods of **monitoring expenditure** and activities against **budgets** are reliable and comply with your organisation's requirements

c) you **monitor expenditure** and activities against agreed **budgets** at appropriate intervals

d) you control **expenditure** in line with **budgets** and the requirements of your organisation

e) you take prompt **corrective action** in response to actual or potential significant variations from **budgets** in line with your organisation's requirements

f) you refer requests for **expenditure** outside your responsibility promptly to the appropriate people

g) your records of activities against **budgets** are complete, accurate and available to authorised people only.

Knowledge requirements

You need to know and understand

Budgets
- the importance of budgetary control to organisational efficiency and your role and responsibility in relation to this
- the principles which underpin effective budgetary control and how to apply them
- the variations from the planned budget which may occur how to identify these and what forms of corrective action you should take in response to them
- the requests for expenditure outside your area of responsibility which may be required and the procedures to follow in response to these

Information handling
- the importance of accurate and comprehensive records of activities against budgets and how to ensure these are kept

Involvement and motivation
- how to encourage and enable team members to take responsibility for monitoring and controlling activities against budgets

Organisational context
- your organisation's requirements for budgetary monitoring and control.

Evidence requirements

You must prove that you *control expenditure and activities against budgets* to the National Standard of competence.

To do this, you must provide evidence to convince your assessor that you consistently meet **all** the performance criteria.

Your evidence must be the result of real work activities undertaken by yourself. Evidence from simulated activities is **not** acceptable for this element.

You must show evidence that you control **both** the following types of **budgets**
- for programmes of work in your area of responsibility
- for the sharing of overhead charges with others.

You must show evidence that you use **two** of the following types of **monitoring**
- considering oral information from others
- examining written information from others, *or*
- examining financial information.

You must show evidence that you control **expenditure** on **two** of the following types of items
- supplies of goods
- supplies of services
- people
- overhead expenses
- capital equipment
- premises.

You must also show evidence that you use **two** of the following types of **corrective action**
- altering activities
- rescheduling expenditure
- altering budget allocations within limits of responsibility
- renegotiating budgets.

You must, however, convince your assessor that you have the necessary knowledge, understanding and skills to be able to perform competently in respect of **all** types of **monitoring**, **expenditure** and **corrective action**, listed above.

Enhance your own performance

Unit summary

This unit is about continuously developing your own knowledge and skills and optimising your use of time and other resources so that you can meet your objectives.

This unit contains two elements

C3.1 *Continuously develop your own knowledge and skills*
C3.2 *Optimise your own resources to meet your objectives.*

Personal competencies

In performing effectively in this unit, you will show that you

Acting assertively
- take personal responsibility for making things happen
- take control of situations and events
- act in an assured and unhesitating manner when faced with a challenge
- say no to unreasonable requests

Communicating
- identify the information needs of listeners
- encourage listeners to ask questions or rephrase statements to clarify their understanding
- modify communication in response to feedback from listeners

Focusing on results
- maintain a focus on objectives
- tackle problems and take advantage of opportunities as they arise
- prioritise objectives and schedule work to make best use of time and resources
- focus personal attention on specific details that are critical to the success of a key event
- establish and communicate high expectations of performance, including setting an example to others
- set goals that are demanding of self and others

Managing self
- take responsibility for meeting your own learning and development needs
- seek feedback on your performance to identify strengths and weaknesses
- change your behaviour where needed as a result of feedback
- reflect systematically on your own performance and modify your behaviour accordingly
- develop yourself to meet the demands of changing situations
- transfer learning from one situation to another

Thinking and taking decisions
- break processes down into tasks and activities
- identify implications, consequences or causal relationships in a situation
- produce a variety of solutions before taking a decision
- take decisions which are realistic for the situation.

**Enhance your own
performance**

Element C3.1

Continuously develop your own knowledge and skills

Performance criteria

You must ensure that

a) you assess your performance and identify your development needs at appropriate intervals

b) your **assessment** takes account of the skills you need to work effectively with other team members

c) you prioritise your development needs so that they are consistent with your current objectives and the likely future requirements of your role

d) your plans for personal development are consistent with the needs you have identified and the resources available

e) your plans for personal development contain specific, measurable, realistic and challenging objectives

f) you obtain support from **relevant people** to help you create learning opportunities

g) you undertake development activities which are consistent with your plans for personal development

h) you obtain feedback from **relevant people** and use it to enhance your performance in the future

i) you update your plans for personal development at appropriate intervals.

Knowledge requirements

You need to know and understand

Communication
- the importance of getting feedback from others on your performance and how to encourage, enable and use such feedback in a constructive manner.

Management competence
- the principal skills required for effective managerial performance
- the types of interpersonal skills required for effective team work.

Organisational context
- the current and likely future requirements and standards within your job role and how they correspond to your level of competence as a manager
- appropriate people from whom to get feedback on your performance

Training and development
- the importance of continuing self-development to managerial competence
- how to assess your own current level of competence
- criteria for prioritising personal development needs
- how to develop a personal action plan for learning and self-development with realistic but challenging objectives
- the types of support which may be available from team members, colleagues, line managers and specialists
- how to identify the need for support, select an appropriate source and obtain required help
- the types of development activities and their relative advantages and disadvantages
- how to assess your personal progress and update your plans accordingly.

Evidence requirements

You must prove that you *continuously develop your own knowledge and skills* to the National Standard of competence.

To do this, you must provide evidence to convince your assessor that you consistently meet **all** the performance criteria.

Your evidence must be the result of real work activities undertaken by yourself. Evidence from simulated activities is **not** acceptable for this element.

You must show evidence that your **assessments** take account of **all** of the following
- work objectives
- personal objectives
- organisational policies and requirements.

You must also show evidence that you obtain support and feedback from at least **two** of the following types of **relevant people**
- team members
- colleagues working at the same level as yourself
- higher-level managers or sponsors
- specialists.

You must, however, convince your assessor that you have the necessary knowledge, understanding and skills to be able to perform competently in respect of **all** types of **relevant people**, listed above.

Enhance your own
performance

Element C3.2

Optimise your own resources to meet your objectives

Performance criteria

You must ensure that

a) you set objectives for your work which are specific, measurable and achievable within **organisational constraints**

b) you prioritise your objectives in line with organisational objectives and policies

c) you plan your work activities so that they are consistent with your objectives and your personal resources

d) your estimates of the time you need for activities are realistic and allow for unforeseen circumstances

e) you **delegate** work to others in a way which makes the most efficient use of available time and resources

f) you take decisions as soon as you have sufficient information

g) when you need further information to take decisions, you take prompt and efficient measures to obtain it

h) you minimise unhelpful interruptions to, and digressions from, planned work

i) you regularly review progress and reschedule activities to help achieve your planned objectives.

Knowledge requirements

You need to know and understand

Delegation
- how to delegate work to others and monitor progress.

Information handling
- how to assess how much information is required before effective decisions can be taken
- how to collect and check the validity of the information required for decision-making.

Monitoring and evaluation
- the importance of regular reviews of activity and rescheduling of work to achieving planned objectives.

Planning
- how to set objectives for yourself which are specific, measurable and achievable
- how to plan activities so that they are consistent with known priorities and your own resources
- how to estimate the amount of time required to carry out planned activities
- the kind of contingencies which may occur and how to assess and plan for these.

Time management
- the importance of effective time management to managerial competence
- how to identify and minimise unhelpful interruptions to planned work.

Evidence requirements

You must prove that you *optimise your own resources to meet your objectives* to the National Standard of competence.

To do this, you must provide evidence to convince your assessor that you consistently meet **all** the performance criteria.

Your evidence must be the result of real work activities undertaken by yourself. Evidence from simulated activities is **not** acceptable for this element.

You must show evidence that, when agreeing your objectives, you take into account **all** the following types of **organisational constraints**
- organisational objectives
- organisational policies
- resources.

You must also show evidence that you can **delegate** to **two** of the following
- team members
- colleagues working at the same level as yourself
- people outside your organisation.

You must, however, convince your assessor that you have the necessary knowledge, understanding and skills to be able to perform competently in respect of **all** types of people to whom you may have to **delegate**, listed above.

Enhance productive working relationships

Unit summary

This unit is about enhancing productive working relationships with your manager and other colleagues in your organisation. It also involves providing guidance on your organisation's values and how to work in accordance with these values.

This unit contains three elements

C6.1 *Enhance the trust and support of colleagues*
C6.2 *Enhance the trust and support of those to whom you report*
C6.3 *Provide guidance on values at work.*

Personal competencies

In performing effectively in this unit, you will show that you

Acting assertively
- act in an assured and unhesitating manner when faced with a challenge
- say no to unreasonable requests
- state your own position and views clearly in conflict situations
- maintain your beliefs, commitment and effort in spite of set-backs or opposition

Behaving ethically
- show integrity and fairness in decision-making
- set objectives and create cultures which are ethical
- clearly identify and raise ethical concerns relevant to your organisation
- work towards the resolution of ethical dilemmas based on reasoned approaches

Building teams
- actively build relationships with others
- make time available to support others
- provide feedback designed to improve people's future performance
- show respect for the views and actions of others
- show sensitivity to the needs and feelings of others
- keep others informed about plans and progress

Communicating
- listen actively, ask questions, clarify points and rephrase others' statements to check mutual understanding
- identify the information needs of listeners
- adopt communication styles appropriate to listeners and situations, including selecting an appropriate time and place

Managing self
- accept personal comments or criticism without becoming defensive
- remain calm in difficult or uncertain situations
- handle others' emotions without becoming personally involved in them

Thinking and taking decisions
- reconcile and make use of a variety of perspectives when making sense of a situation
- produce your own ideas from experience and practice
- take decisions which are realistic for the situation
- focus on facts, problems and solutions when handling an emotional situation.

Enhance productive working relationships

Element C6.1

Enhance the trust and support of colleagues

Performance criteria

You must ensure that

a) you consult with **colleagues** about proposed activities at appropriate times and in a manner which encourages open, frank discussion

b) you keep **colleagues** informed about organisational plans and activities, emerging threats and opportunities

c) you honour the commitments you make to **colleagues**

d) you treat **colleagues** in a manner which shows your respect for individuals and the need for confidentiality

e) you give **colleagues** sufficient support for them to achieve their work objectives

f) you discuss directly with the **colleagues** concerned your evaluation of their work and behaviour.

Knowledge requirements

You need to know and understand

Communication

- how to consult with colleagues in a way which encourages open and frank discussions
- how to select communication methods appropriate to the issues and contexts
- the importance of effective communication methods to productive working relationships
- the importance of discussing evaluations of output and behaviour at work promptly and directly with those concerned
- how to provide feedback in a way which will lead to a constructive outcome.

Information handling

- the types of information concerning colleagues which need to be treated confidentially and procedures to follow to ensure this.

Organisational context

- the organisational plans and activities, emerging threats and opportunities, which are relevant to the work of colleagues and about which they need to be informed.

Providing support

- the support colleagues may require to achieve their objectives and how to provide such support.

Working relationships

- how people work in groups especially at senior levels within an organisation
- the strategies and styles of working which encourage effective working relationships
- the importance of honouring commitments to colleagues
- the importance of showing respect for colleagues and how to do this.

Evidence requirements

You must prove that you *enhance the trust and support of colleagues* to the National Standard of competence.

To do this, you must provide evidence to convince your assessor that you consistently meet **all** the performance criteria.

Your evidence must be the result of real work activities undertaken by yourself. Evidence from simulated activities is **not** acceptable for this element.

You must show evidence of gaining the trust and support of **two** of the following types of **colleagues**

- those working at the same level as you
- those working at a higher level than you
- those working at a lower level than you.

You must, however, convince your assessor that you have the necessary knowledge, understanding and skills to be able to perform competently in respect of **all** types of **colleagues**, listed above.

Enhance productive working
relationships

Element C6.2

Enhance the trust and support of those to whom you report

Performance criteria

You must ensure that

a) you give **those to whom you report** timely and accurate reports on activities, progress, results and achievements

b) you give **those to whom you report** clear and accurate information about emerging threats and opportunities with a degree of urgency appropriate to the situation

c) your **proposals** for action are clear and realistic

d) you present your **proposals** for action to **those to whom you report** at appropriate times

e) where you have disagreements with **those to whom you report**, you make constructive efforts to resolve these disagreements and maintain good working relationships.

Knowledge requirements

You need to know and understand

Communication

- the importance of keeping those to whom you report informed of activities, progress, results and achievements and how to do this
- how to develop and present proposals in ways which are realistic, clear and likely to influence those to whom you report positively.

Organisational context

- the management structures, lines of accountability and control in your organisation
- the general responsibilities of those to whom you report
- the decision making processes within your organisation
- the types of emerging threats and opportunities about which those to whom you report need to be informed and the degree of urgency attached to these
- the types of organisational policies and ways of working about which you need to consult with those to whom you report, and how to do this.

Working relationships

- strategies and styles of working which encourage effective working relationships
- methods of handling disagreements with those to whom you report in a constructive manner.

Evidence requirements

You must prove that you *enhance the trust and support of those to whom you report* to the National Standard of competence.

To do this, you must provide evidence to convince your assessor that you consistently meet **all** the performance criteria.

Your evidence must be the result of real work activities undertaken by yourself. Evidence from simulated activities is acceptable **only** for performance criterion e) in this element.

You must show evidence that you gain the support of **one** of **those to whom you report** who is either

- an individual
- an organisation, board or other authority.

You must also show evidence that you present **proposals** in **one** of the following forms

- spoken
- written.

You must, however, convince your assessor that you have the necessary knowledge, understanding and skills to be able to perform competently in respect of **all** types of **those to whom you report** and **proposals**, listed above.

Enhance productive working relationships

Element C6.3

Provide guidance on values at work

Performance criteria

You must ensure that

a) you consult with **relevant people** on the way in which values are expressed in work and working relationships

b) you provide clear and relevant **guidance** on organisational values and the limits of acceptable practice

c) where problems and conflicts arise which cannot be addressed routinely, you provide adequate resources to resolve the situation promptly

d) where activities contradict organisational values and **guidance**, you impose disciplinary sanctions in line with organisational policies and legal requirements.

Knowledge requirements

You need to know and understand

Communication
- how to consult with team members, colleagues, line managers and personnel specialists on values issues.

Organisational context
- the values of your organisation
- how to interpret organisational values and identify the implications for behaviour at work and in working relationships
- the types of breaches of organisational values and guidance which could occur and what kind of responses to these are appropriate according to organisational policy and legal requirements.

Working relationships
- the importance of values to organisations and the contribution they can make to the work of staff and overall organisational effectiveness
- the types of guidance which team members, colleagues, line managers and personnel specialists may require on organisational values and the limits of acceptable practice and how to provide this guidance
- the types of problems and conflicts which may arise concerning the application of values within the organisation and strategies to resolve these.

Evidence requirements

You must prove that you *provide guidance on values at work* to the National Standard of competence.

To do this, you must provide evidence to convince your assessor that you consistently meet **all** the performance criteria.

Your evidence must be the result of real work activities undertaken by yourself. Evidence from simulated activities is acceptable **only** for performance criteria c) and d) in this element.

You must show evidence of consulting with, and providing guidance to, **two** of the following types of **relevant people**
- team members
- colleagues working at the same level as yourself
- higher-level managers or sponsors
- specialists.

You must also show evidence of providing **two** of the following types of **guidance**
- individual counselling
- group discussions
- training programmes
- publication of guidance materials.

You must, however, convince your assessor that you have the necessary knowledge, understanding and skills to be able to perform competently in respect of **all** types of **relevant people** and **guidance** listed above.

Use information to take critical decisions

Unit summary

This unit is about using information so that you can take critical decisions effectively. It covers obtaining relevant information, analysing this information, and taking decisions which are critical to your organisation's performance. It also covers advising and informing other people.

This unit contains four elements

D6.1   *Obtain the information needed to take critical decisions*
D6.2   *Analyse information for decision making*
D6.3   *Take critical decisions*
D6.4   *Advise and inform others.*

Personal competencies

In performing effectively in this unit, you will show that you

Acting strategically
- clearly relate your goals and actions to the strategic aims of your organisation
- take opportunities when they arise to achieve the longer term aims or needs of your organisation

Communicating
- listen actively, ask questions, clarify points and rephrase others' statements to check mutual understanding
- adopt communication styles appropriate to listeners and situations, including selecting an appropriate time and place
- encourage listeners to ask questions or rephrase statements to clarify their understanding

Influencing others
- present yourself positively to others
- create and prepare strategies for influencing others
- use a variety of means to influence others
- understand the culture of your organisation and act to work within it or influence it

Searching for information
- establish information networks to search for and gather relevant information
- make best use of existing sources of information
- seek information from multiple sources
- challenge the validity and reliability of sources of information
- push for concrete information in an ambiguous situation

Thinking and taking decisions
- break processes down into tasks and activities
- identify implications, consequences or causal relationships in a situation
- identify patterns or meaning from events and data which are not obviously related
- build a total and valid picture from restricted or incomplete data
- produce a variety of solutions before taking a decision
- balance intuition with logic in decision making
- reconcile and make use of a variety of perspectives when making sense of a situation
- produce your own ideas from experience and practice
- take decisions which are realistic for the situation
- take decisions in uncertain situations or based on restricted information when necessary.

Use information to take critical
decisions

Element D6.1

Obtain the information needed to take critical decisions

Performance criteria

You must ensure that

a) you identify the **information** you need
   to make the required **decisions**

b) the **sources** from which you gather
   information are reliable and
   sufficiently wide-ranging to meet your
   information needs

c) your **methods of obtaining
   information** are reliable, effective and
   make efficient use of resources

d) your **methods of obtaining
   information** are consistent with
   organisational values, policies and legal
   requirements

e) the **information** you obtain is accurate,
   relevant and sufficient to allow you to
   take **decisions**

f) where **information** is inadequate,
   contradictory or ambiguous, you take
   prompt and effective action to deal with
   this.

Knowledge requirements

You need to know and understand

Analytical techniques
- how to identify the information you need to take critical decisions effectively
- how to judge the accuracy, relevance and sufficiency of information you need to take decisions in different contexts
- how to identify information which may be contradictory, ambiguous or inadequate and how to deal with these problems

Information handling
- the importance of information management to the team and to organisational effectiveness and your role and responsibilities in relation to this
- the types of qualitative and quantitative information which are essential to your role and responsibilities, and how to identify these
- the range of sources of information which are available to you and how to ensure that these are capable of meeting current and likely future information requirements
- how to identify new sources of information which may be required
- the range of methods of gathering and checking the validity of such information and their advantages and disadvantages

Organisational context
- the organisational values and policies and the legal requirements which have a bearing on the collection of information and how to interpret these.

Evidence requirements

You must prove that you *obtain the information needed to take critical decisions* to the National Standard of competence.

To do this, you must provide evidence to convince your assessor that you consistently meet **all** the performance criteria.

Your evidence must be the result of real work activities undertaken by yourself. Evidence from simulated activities is **not** acceptable for this element.

You must show evidence that you use at least **three** of the following types of **sources** of information
- people within your organisation
- people outside your organisation
- internal information systems
- published media
- specially commissioned research.

You must show evidence that you obtain **both** of the following types of **information**
- quantitative
- qualitative.

You must show evidence that you use **four** of the following types of **methods of obtaining information**
- listening and watching
- reading
- spoken questioning
- written questioning
- formal research conducted personally
- formal research conducted by third parties.

You must also show evidence that you take at least **one** of the following types of **decisions**
- affecting operational performance
- affecting organisational policy.

You must, however, convince your assessor that you have the necessary knowledge, understanding and skills to be able to perform competently in respect of **all** types of **sources of information, methods of obtaining information** and **decisions** listed above.

Use information to take critical decisions

Element D6.2

Analyse information for decision making

Performance criteria

You must ensure that

a) you identify objectives for your **analysis** which are clear and consistent with the **decisions** you need to make

b) you select **information** which is accurate, relevant to the objectives, and sufficient to arrive at reliable **decisions**

c) you use methods of **analysis** which are suitable to achieve the objectives

d) your **analysis** of the **information** correctly identifies patterns and trends significant to the **decisions** you need to take

e) you develop clear conclusions which you support with reasoned arguments and appropriate evidence

f) in presenting the results of your **analysis**, you differentiate clearly between fact and opinion

g) your records of your **analysis** are sufficient to show the assumptions and **decisions** made at each stage.

Knowledge requirements

You need to know and understand

Analytical techniques

- different approaches to, and methods of, analysing information and how to select methods appropriate to decisions which you have to make
- how to analyse information to identify patterns and trends
- how to draw conclusions on the basis of analysing information
- the differences between fact and opinion – how to identify these and present them accordingly

Communication

- how to develop and present a reasoned logical case based on the outcomes of an analysis

Information handling

- the importance of the effective analysis of information and your role and responsibility in relation to this
- types of information, both qualitative and quantitative, which you need to analyse
- how to select information relevant to the decisions you need to make and ensure such information is accurate and relevant
- the importance of record-keeping to the analysis of information and how such records should be kept and used.

Evidence requirements

You must prove that you *analyse information for decision making* to the National Standard of competence.

To do this, you must provide evidence to convince your assessor that you consistently meet **all** the performance criteria.

Your evidence must be the result of real work activities undertaken by yourself. Evidence from simulated activities is **not** acceptable for this element.

You must show evidence that you carry out **both** of the following types of **analysis**

- formal and planned
- informal and ad hoc.

You must also show evidence that you take at least **one** of the following types of **decisions**

- affecting operational performance
- affecting organisational policy.

You must also show evidence that you use **both** of the following types of **information**

- qualitative
- quantitative.

You must, however, convince your assessor that you have the necessary knowledge, understanding and skills to be able to perform competently in taking **both** types of **decisions** listed above.

UNIT D6

Use information to take critical decisions

Element D6.3

Take critical decisions

Performance criteria

You must ensure that

a) your **decisions** are based on sufficient, valid and reliable **information** and analysis

b) your **decisions** are consistent with organisational values, policies, guidelines and procedures

c) you obtain advice from **relevant people** if there is insufficient **information** or your **decisions** conflict with organisational values, policies, guidelines and procedures

d) you take **decisions** in time for appropriate action to be taken

e) you communicate your **decisions** to those who need to know.

Knowledge requirements

You need to know and understand

Analytical techniques
- how to decide when you have sufficient, valid and reliable information to be able to take a decision
- how to test the validity and reliability of information
- how to check that your decisions are consistent with the information available and your analysis
- how to justify your decisions

Communication
- the people who need to be informed about your decisions and how to ensure this happens

Organisational context
- relevant organisational values, policies, guidelines and procedures
- people from whom to seek advice if you have insufficient information or if there is a conflict
- the actions which need to be taken as a result of the decision and when these actions need to be taken.

Evidence requirements

You must prove that you *take critical decisions* to the National Standard of competence.

To do this, you must provide evidence to convince your assessor that you consistently meet **all** the performance criteria.

Your evidence must be the result of real work activities undertaken by yourself. Evidence from simulated activities is **not** acceptable for this element.

You must also show evidence that you take at least **one** of the following types of **decisions**
- affecting operational performance
- affecting organisational policy.

You must also show evidence that you seek advice from at least **two** of the following types of **relevant people**
- colleagues working at the same level as yourself
- higher-level managers or sponsors
- specialists.

You must also show evidence that you use **both** of the following types of **information**
- qualitative
- quantitative.

You must, however, convince your assessor that you have the necessary knowledge, understanding and skills to be able to perform competently in respect of **all** types of **decisions** and **relevant people** listed above.

Use information to take critical decisions

Element D6.4

Advise and inform others

Performance criteria

You must ensure that

a) you research the **advice and information** needs of your **recipients** in ways which are appropriate and sufficient and take account of your **organisational constraints**

b) you provide **advice and information** at a time and place and in a **form** and manner appropriate to the needs of your **recipients**

c) the **information** you provide is accurate, current, relevant and sufficient

d) your **advice** is consistent with organisational policy, procedures and **constraints**

e) your **advice** is supported by reasoned arguments and appropriate evidence

f) you confirm your **recipients'** understanding of the **advice and information** you have given

g) you maintain confidentiality according to organisational and legal requirements

h) you use feedback from **recipients** to improve the way you provide **advice and information**.

Knowledge requirements

You need to know and understand

Communication

- how to communicate advice and information effectively both through speaking and in writing
- how to develop and present a reasoned case when providing advice to others
- the importance of confirming the recipient's understanding of information and advice provided and how to do this
- the importance of providing advice and information and your role and responsibilities in relation to this
- the types of advice and information which people may require
- how to identify information needs
- the situations in which it is appropriate to act on one's own initiative in giving information and advice
- the importance of seeking feedback on the quality and relevance of the advice and information you provide and how to encourage such feedback

Information handling

- the importance of checking the validity of advice and information provided to others
- how to ensure accuracy, currency, sufficiency and relevance of advice and information
- the principles of confidentiality when handling information and advice – what types of information and advice may be provided to what people

Organisational context

- organisational policies, procedures and resource constraints which may affect advice given to others.

Evidence requirements

You must prove that you *advise and inform others* to the National Standard of competence.

To do this, you must provide evidence to convince your assessor that you consistently meet **all** the performance criteria.

Your evidence must be the result of real work activities undertaken by yourself. Evidence from simulated activities is **not** acceptable for this element.

You must show evidence that you provide **both** of the following types of **forms** of advice and information
- spoken
- written.

You must show evidence that you provide **advice and information** in **both** of the following circumstances
- in response to a request
- on your own initiative.

You must show evidence that you provide information and advice to at least **two** of the following types of **recipients**
- team members
- colleagues working at the same level
- higher-level managers and sponsors
- people outside your organisation.

You must also show evidence that you take account of **all** of the following types of **organisational constraints**
- organisational objectives
- organisational policies
- resources.

You must, however, convince your assessor that you have the necessary knowledge, understanding and skills to be able to perform competently in respect of **all** types of **recipients** listed above.

Operational Management

Level 5

NVQ/SVQ

Optional units
Candidates take FOUR optional units

Secure financial resources for your organisation's plans

Unit summary

This unit is about managing your organisation's finance at a strategic level. It covers examining the way your organisation generates and allocates financial resources, evaluating proposals from others on expenditure, and obtaining the financial resources which your organisation needs.

This unit contains three elements

B5.1 *Review the generation and allocation of financial resources*
B5.2 *Evaluate proposals for expenditure*
B5.3 *Obtain financial resources for your organisation's activities.*

Personal competencies

In performing effectively in this unit, you will show that you

Acting strategically
- display an understanding of how the different parts of the organisation and its environment fit together
- work towards a clearly defined vision of the future
- clearly relate your goals and actions to the strategic aims of your organisation
- take opportunities when they arise to achieve the longer-term aims or needs of your organisation

Communicating
- listen actively, ask questions, clarify points and rephrase others' statements and check mutual understanding
- adopt communication styles appropriate to listeners and situations, including selecting an appropriate time and place

Influencing others
- develop and use contacts to trade information, and obtain support and resources
- present yourself positively to others
- create and prepare strategies for influencing others
- understand the culture of your organisation and act to work within it or influence it

Searching for information
- actively encourage the free exchange of information
- make best use of existing sources of information
- seek information from multiple sources
- challenge the validity and reliability of sources of information
- push for concrete information in an ambiguous situation

Thinking and taking decisions
- break processes down into tasks and activities
- identify patterns or meaning from events and data which are not obviously related
- produce a variety of solutions before taking a decision
- take decisions which are realistic for the situation.

Secure financial resources for
your organisation's plans

Element B5.1

Review the generation and allocation of financial resources

Performance criteria

You must ensure that

a) your systems for reviewing the **generation** and **allocation of financial resources** provide accurate, comprehensive and up-to-date information

b) the criteria you use for assessing the organisation's performance in the **generation** and **allocation of financial resources** take account of the type of organisation, its context and culture

c) the criteria you use include commonly accepted performance measures for the **generation** and **allocation of financial resources**

d) your review shows how well the organisation is performing compared with other organisations

e) your review shows how effective the organisation's methods are compared to alternative methods of **generation** and **allocation of financial resources**

f) you gather, store and use information on the **generation** and **allocation of financial resources** in accordance with organisational policies and legal requirements.

Knowledge requirements

You need to know and understand

Legal requirements

- legal requirements for the handling of information on the generation and allocation of financial resources

Monitoring and evaluation

- systems which may be used to review the generation and allocation of financial resources and their relative advantages and disadvantages to your area of work and available resources
- the information which is needed to review the generation and allocation of financial resources and how to collect this information
- how to select criteria which are appropriate to your organisation, its context and culture
- the commonly accepted performance measures for the generation and allocation of financial resources
- how to compare your organisation's performance with that of others
- alternative methods of generating and allocating financial resources which may be appropriate and how to evaluate these

Organisational context

- the context and culture of the organisation and the implications of these for resource generation and allocation
- organisational requirements for the handling of information
- other organisations against which it is appropriate to compare your organisation's performance

Resource management

- the importance of continuously reviewing the generation and allocation of financial resources and your role and responsibilities in this regard.

Evidence requirements

You must prove that you *review the generation and allocation of financial resources* to the National Standard of competence.

To do this, you must provide evidence to convince your assessor that you consistently meet **all** the performance criteria.

Your evidence must be the result of real work activities undertaken by yourself. Evidence from simulated activities is **not** acceptable for this element.

You must show evidence that you review at least **two** of the following methods for the **generation of financial resources**

- raising equity finance
- obtaining loans
- obtaining venture capital
- negotiating with government for funds
- obtaining sponsorship
- creative and innovative approaches.

You must also show evidence that you review at least **one** of the following methods for the **allocation of financial resources**

- budgeted plans
- internal bidding and departmental competition or collaboration
- external bidding and interorganisational competition or collaboration.

You must, however, convince your assessor that you have the necessary knowledge, understanding and skills to be able to perform competently in respect of **all** types of **generation** and **allocation of financial resources,** listed above.

Secure financial resources for your organisation's plans

Element B5.2

Evaluate proposals for expenditure

Performance criteria

You must ensure that

a) you select **evaluation** criteria which are relevant, fair and clear

b) you provide those submitting **proposals** with sufficient help to make their **proposals** effective

c) you **evaluate proposals** against your stated criteria within the agreed timescale

d) you **evaluate proposals** for their expected benefits and costs, and according to how realistic and achievable these benefits and costs appear to be

e) the **proposals** you accept clearly show how they support the organisation's objectives, strategies, values and policies

f) you highlight weaknesses or inconsistencies in **proposals** and form a justifiable case for rejection or amendment

g) you clearly explain the reasons for the rejection or amendment of **proposals** to those submitting the **proposals**

h) you conduct negotiations over **proposals** in a manner likely to ensure the co-operation, confidence and goodwill of the people involved.

Knowledge requirements

You need to know and understand

Communication
- how to develop and present a case for the acceptance or rejection of proposals

Monitoring and evaluation
- the range of criteria for evaluating proposals for expenditure and their relative advantages and disadvantages to your role and responsibilities
- how to evaluate proposals against selected criteria and carry out cost-benefit analyses of these
- what weaknesses and inconsistencies may be present in proposals and how to identify and evaluate these

Organisational context
- your organisation's objectives, strategies, values and policies relevant to evaluating proposals for expenditure

Providing support
- the types of help those making proposals may need and how to provide support effectively

Resource management
- why the thorough evaluation of proposals for expenditure is essential and your role and responsibilities in relation to this

Working relationships
- strategies to use when carrying out negotiations on expenditure proposals so that the co-operation, confidence and goodwill of those involved is maintained.

Evidence requirements

You must prove that you *evaluate proposals for expenditure* to the National Standard of competence.

To do this, you must provide evidence to convince your assessor that you consistently meet **all** the performance criteria.

Your evidence must be the result of real work activities undertaken by yourself. Evidence from simulated activities is **not** acceptable for this element.

You must show evidence that you use **one** of the following types of **evaluation**
- comparative
- absolute.

You must also show evidence that you evaluate **all** of the following types of **proposals**
- for long-term programmes of work
- for medium-term programmes of work
- for short-term programmes of work.

You must, however, convince your assessor that you have the necessary knowledge, understanding and skills to be able to perform competently in respect of **all** types of **evaluation**, listed above.

Secure financial resources for
your organisation's plans

Element B5.3

Obtain financial resources for your organisation's activities

Performance criteria

You must ensure that

a) you give opportunities to **relevant people** to help to obtain financial resources for your organisation's activities

b) the case you make for obtaining resources is clear, consistent and supported by sound argument

c) the way you present your case reflects the commitment of those who will be using the resources

d) your **activities to obtain resources** are consistent with the good name and image of your organisation and with legal requirements

e) when the resources you need are not obtained in full, you agree realistic alternative courses of action with **relevant people**

f) all your agreements, communications and other **activities to obtain resources** are consistent with the mission, values and policies of the organisation.

Knowledge requirements

You need to know and understand

Involvement and motivation
- how to encourage and enable team members, colleagues and line managers to help to obtain financial resources for your organisation's work
- how to develop and present a case for obtaining financial resources in a way which is likely to gain the support of key decision makers

Legal requirements
- legislation relevant to obtaining financial resources

Organisational context
- the relevant aspects of the organisation's mission, values and policies which may affect agreements and communications concerning the obtaining of financial resources
- how to interpret these and ensure compliance with them

Resource management
- the range of activities to obtain financial resources and their relative advantages and disadvantages in relation to your organisation
- the importance of having alternative methods of obtaining resources and how to identify and evaluate them.

Evidence requirements

You must prove that you *obtain financial resources for the organisation's activities* to the National Standard of competence.

To do this, you must provide evidence to convince your assessor that you consistently meet **all** the performance criteria.

Your evidence must be the result of real work activities undertaken by yourself. Evidence from simulated activities is **not** acceptable for this element.

You must show evidence that you involve at least **two** of the following types of **relevant people**
- team members
- colleagues working at the same level
- higher-level managers or sponsors.

You must also show evidence that you use at least **two** of the following types of **activities to obtain resources**
- formal proposals
- consultation
- lobbying
- private discussion
- media usage
- publishing documents.

You must, however, convince your assessor that you have the necessary knowledge, understanding and skills to be able to perform competently in respect of **all** types of **relevant people** and **activities to obtain resources,** listed above.

Select personnel for activities

Unit summary

This unit is about recruiting and selecting the people you need to carry out your work activities. It applies to both external and internal recruitment of people for permanent work, temporary work or project work. It applies equally to paid or voluntary work, whether full-time or part-time.

This unit contains two elements

C8.1 *Identify personnel requirements*
C8.2 *Select required personnel.*

Personal competencies

In performing effectively in this unit, you will show that you

Acting assertively
- state your own position and views clearly in conflict situations
- maintain your own beliefs, commitment and effort in spite of set-backs and opposition

Behaving ethically
- comply with legislation, industry regulation, professional and organisational codes
- show integrity and fairness in decision-making

Communicating
- listen actively, ask questions, clarify points and rephrase others' statements and check mutual understanding
- adopt communication styles appropriate to listeners and situations, including selecting an appropriate time and place
- confirm listeners' understanding through questioning and interpretation of non-verbal signals
- encourage listeners to ask questions or rephrase statements to clarify their understanding
- modify communication in response to feedback from listeners

Influencing others
- present yourself positively to others
- create and prepare strategies for influencing others
- understand the culture of your organisation and act to work within it or influence it

Searching for information
- actively encourage the free exchange of information
- make best use of existing sources of information
- seek information from multiple sources
- challenge the validity and reliability of sources of information
- push for concrete information in an ambiguous situation

Thinking and taking decisions
- break processes down into tasks and activities
- identify patterns or meaning from events and data which are not obviously related
- take decisions which are realistic for the situation.

Select personnel for activities

Element C8.1

Identify personnel requirements

Performance criteria

You must ensure that

a) you clearly and accurately identify the organisational objectives and constraints affecting **personnel** requirements

b) you consult with relevant people on **personnel** requirements in a timely and confidential manner

c) your estimates of **personnel** requirements are based on an accurate analysis of sufficient, up-to-date and reliable information

d) the **specifications** you develop are clear, accurate and comply with organisational and legal requirements

e) the **specifications** you develop identify fair and objective criteria for selection

f) the **specifications** you develop are agreed with **authorised people** prior to recruitment action.

Knowledge requirements

You need to know and understand

Communication

- how to make a case for additional personnel requirements in a way which is likely to influence decision-makers positively.

Information handling

- how to collect and validate the information needed to specify personnel requirements.

Involvement and motivation

- the issues for which consultation with relevant people may be necessary and how to do so
- the importance of agreeing personnel requirements in advance with relevant people.

Legal requirements

- the legal requirements for the specification of personnel requirements.

Organisational context

- the work objectives and constraints which have a bearing on identifying personnel requirements.

Recruitment and selection

- the methods of specifying personnel requirements and their relative advantages and disadvantages to your work
- how to identify personnel needs for your team and specify job roles, competences and attributes required to meet these needs
- the types of information necessary to specify personnel requirements
- how to identify fair and objective criteria for the selection of staff.

Evidence requirements

You must prove that you *identify personnel requirements* to the National Standard of competence.

To do this, you must provide evidence to convince your assessor that you consistently meet **all** the performance criteria.

Your evidence must be the result of real work activities undertaken by yourself. Evidence from simulated activities is **not** acceptable for this element.

You must show evidence that you identify requirements for at least **four** of the following types of **personnel**

- internal
- external
- permanent
- temporary
- full-time
- part-time
- paid
- voluntary.

You must also show evidence that you involve at least **two** of the following types of **authorised people**

- team members
- colleagues working at the same level as yourself
- higher-level managers or sponsors
- personnel specialists
- members of the selection team.

You must also show evidence that you develop **all** of the following types of **specifications**

- key purpose of the posts
- individual and team roles and responsibilities
- required individual and team competencies
- other details specific to the organisation.

You must, however, convince your assessor that you have the necessary knowledge, understanding and skills to be able to perform competently in respect of **all** types of **personnel** and **authorised people**, listed above.

Select personnel for activities

Element C8.2

Select required personnel

Performance criteria

You must ensure that

a) you use appropriately skilled and experienced people to assess and select **personnel**

b) the **information** you obtain about each candidate is relevant to and sufficient for the selection process

c) you assess the **information** objectively against specified selection criteria

d) your selection decisions are justifiable from the evidence gained

e) you only inform authorised people about selection decisions and the identified development needs of successful candidates

f) the **information** you provide to authorised people is clear and accurate

g) all candidates receive feedback and **information** appropriate to their needs at each stage of the selection process

h) your records of the selection process are complete, accurate, clear and comply with organisational and legal requirements

i) you pass on your recommendations for improvements to the selection process to the appropriate people in your organisation.

Knowledge requirements

You need to know and understand

Communication
- how to present and justify selection decisions
- how to communicate selection decisions.

Continuous improvement
- the importance of continually reviewing your selection processes and how to do so
- how to make a case for change in selection processes.

Information handling
- the importance of confidentiality during the selection process
- the importance of accurate record-keeping during the selection process.

Legal requirements
- the legal requirements for the selection of personnel

Organisational context
- the organisational requirements for the selection of personnel.

Recruitment and selection
- the relative advantages and disadvantages of the range of methods which may be used for the assessment and selection of staff to your work
- the skills and experience staff need to take part in selection processes
- the information you need to select personnel
- how to make fair and objective assessments
- how to identify the additional development needs of those you select and what to do with this information
- why all candidates should receive feedback at appropriate points during the selection process.

Evidence requirements

You must prove that you *select required personnel* to the National Standard of competence.

To do this, you must provide evidence to convince your assessor that you consistently meet **all** the performance criteria.

Your evidence must be the result of real work activities undertaken by yourself. Evidence from simulated activities is **not** acceptable for this element.

You must show evidence that you select at least **four** of the following types of **personnel**

- internal
- external
- permanent
- temporary
- full-time
- part-time
- paid
- voluntary.

You must also show evidence that you obtain and assess at least **four** of the following types of **information**
- biographical data
- letters
- references
- interview responses
- presentations
- results of work skill tests
- results of knowledge tests.

You must, however, convince your assessor that you have the necessary knowledge, understanding and skills to be able to perform competently in respect of **all** types of **personnel** and **information**, listed above.

Develop teams and individuals to enhance performance

Unit summary

This unit is about developing your team's skills and knowledge to ensure the best possible results at work. It covers identifying the development needs of your team and its members, planning their development and using a variety of activities to improve team performance. It also covers your role in supporting individuals' learning, assessing teams and individuals against agreed development objectives, and continually improving development activities, policies and overall practice.

This unit contains six elements

C10.1 *Identify the development needs of teams and individuals*
C10.2 *Plan the development of teams and individuals*
C10.3 *Develop teams to improve performance*
C10.4 *Support individual learning and development*
C10.5 *Assess the development of teams and individuals*
C10.6 *Improve the development of teams and individuals.*

Personal competencies

In performing effectively in this unit, you will show that you

Acting assertively
- state your own position and views clearly in conflict situations
- maintain your beliefs, commitment and effort in spite of set-backs or opposition

Building teams
- make time available to support others
- encourage and stimulate others to make the best use of their abilities
- evaluate and enhance people's capability to do their jobs
- provide feedback designed to improve people's future performance
- use power and authority in a fair and equitable manner
- invite others to contribute to planning and organising work
- set objectives which are both achievable and challenging

Communicating
- listen actively, ask questions, clarify points and rephrase others' statements to check mutual understanding
- identify the information needs of listeners
- adopt communication styles appropriate to listeners and situations, including selecting an appropriate time and place
- use a variety of media and communication aids to reinforce points and maintain interest
- present difficult ideas and problems in ways that promote understanding
- confirm listeners' understanding through questioning and interpretation of non-verbal signals
- encourage listeners to ask questions or rephrase statements to clarify their understanding
- modify communication in response to feedback from listeners

Thinking and taking decisions
- break processes down into tasks and activities
- use your own experience and evidence from others to identify problems and understand situations
- take decisions which are realistic for the situation.

Develop teams and individuals
to enhance performance

Element C10.1

Identify the development needs of teams and individuals

Performance criteria

You must ensure that

a) you give opportunities to team members to help identify their own **development needs** and those of the team as a whole

b) you identify **development needs** accurately and base your decisions on sufficient reliable and valid information

c) you identify **development needs** for all the **personnel** you are responsible for

d) where required, you seek guidance from competent **specialists**

e) you provide information on **development needs** to authorised people only, in the format required and to agreed deadlines

f) your records of identified **development needs** comply with organisational procedures.

Knowledge requirements

You need to know and understand

Communication

- how to present development needs to relevant people in a way which is likely to influence their decision-making positively.

Continuous improvement

- the importance of human resource development to organisational effectiveness.

Equal opportunities

- the importance of equality of opportunity in human resource development.

Information handling

- how to collect and validate the information you need to identify development needs
- the importance of good record-keeping.

Involvement and motivation

- the importance of providing your team members with opportunities to identify their own development needs and those of the team as a whole
- how to encourage and enable team members to identify development needs.

Organisational context

- the team objectives and organisational values which have a bearing on the identification of training needs.

Training and development

- how to identify development needs for your team and the information needed to do so
- the types of support and guidance which may be needed from specialists and how to get them.

Evidence requirements

You must prove that you *identify the development needs of teams and individuals* to the National Standard of competence.

To do this, you must provide evidence to convince your assessor that you consistently meet **all** the performance criteria.

Your evidence must be the result of real work activities undertaken by yourself. Evidence from simulated activities is **only** acceptable for performance criterion d) in this element.

You must show evidence that you identify **both** of the following types of **development needs**

- to meet organisational objectives
- to meet individual aspirations.

You must also show evidence that you identify development needs for at least **four** of the following types of **personnel**

- internal
- external
- permanent
- temporary
- full-time
- part-time
- paid
- voluntary.

You must also show evidence that you seek guidance from at least **one** of the following types of **specialists**

- within your organisation
- from outside your organisation.

You must, however, convince your assessor that you have the necessary knowledge, understanding and skills to be able to perform competently in respect of **all** aspects of **personnel** and **specialists**, listed above.

Develop teams and individuals
to enhance performance

Element C10.2

Plan the development of teams and individuals

Performance criteria

You must ensure that

a) your plans reflect the identified training and development needs of all the **personnel** you are responsible for

b) your plans contain clear, relevant and realistic development objectives

c) your plans clearly identify the processes you will use and the resources you need

d) your plans are capable of being implemented within the defined timescales

e) where resources are insufficient to meet all identified needs, your plans accurately reflect organisational priorities

f) you present your plans to **relevant people** in an appropriate and timely manner

g) you update your plans at regular intervals after discussion and agreement with **relevant people**.

Knowledge requirements

You need to know and understand

Communication
- how to present your plans in a way which will positively influence the decision-making of relevant people.

Equal opportunities
- the importance of equality of opportunity in planning the development of team members.

Involvement and motivation
- the importance of agreeing development plans with those involved, and processes which may be used to achieve such agreement.

Organisational context
- the correct procedures for presenting plans for the development of teams and individuals.

Planning
- the importance of effective planning to human resource development
- the principles of good practice which underpin human resource development planning
- how to develop effective and realistic plans for individual and team development.

Training and development
- the team development needs which you have identified, and how your plans will help to meet these
- the importance of prioritising development activities and how to do this.

Evidence requirements

You must prove that you *plan the development of teams and individuals* to the National Standard of competence.

To do this, you must provide evidence to convince your assessor that you consistently meet **all** the performance criteria.

Your evidence must be the result of real work activities undertaken by yourself. Evidence from simulated activities is **only** acceptable for performance criterion e) in this element.

You must show evidence that your plans meet the development needs for at least **four** of the following types of **personnel**
- internal
- external
- permanent
- temporary
- full-time
- part-time
- paid
- voluntary.

You must also show evidence that you present your plans to at least **two** of the following types of **relevant people**
- team members
- colleagues working at the same level as yourself
- higher-level managers or sponsors
- specialists.

You must, however, convince your assessor that you have the necessary knowledge, understanding and skills to be able to perform competently in respect of **all** types of **personnel** and **relevant people**, listed above.

Develop teams and individuals
to enhance performance

Element C10.3

Develop teams to improve performance

Performance criteria

You must ensure that

a) the **development activities** which you organise support your team and organisational objectives

b) the **development activities** which you organise make best use of available resources

c) you provide all team members with equal access to relevant **development activities**

d) you demonstrate your own commitment to individual and team development through your personal support for, and involvement in, the **development activities**.

Knowledge requirements

You need to know and understand

Equal opportunities
- the importance of equality of opportunity in implementing development activities and how to ensure this.

Involvement and motivation
- how to motivate staff and win their commitment to, and participation in, development activities.

Leadership styles
- the importance of showing your own commitment to development activities
- how to present a positive role model in this regard to team members.

Training and development
- the range of activities which you may use to develop your team
- how to select and implement development activities which are appropriate to the team members, their development needs and work, the context in which you are operating and the available resources
- how to ensure that development activities meet agreed objectives and plans.

Evidence requirements

You must prove that you *develop teams to improve performance* to the National Standard of competence.

To do this, you must provide evidence to convince your assessor that you consistently meet **all** the performance criteria.

Your evidence must be the result of real work activities undertaken by yourself. Evidence from simulated activities is **not** acceptable for this element.

You must show evidence that you use at least **two** of the following types of **development activities**
- naturally occurring learning opportunities at work
- specifically designed learning opportunities at work
- formal training
- informal training.

You must, however, convince your assessor that you have the necessary knowledge, understanding and skills to be able to perform competently in respect of **all** types of **development activities**, listed above.

Develop teams and individuals
to enhance performance

Element C10.4

Support individual learning and development

Performance criteria

You must ensure that:

a) the **support** you provide is consistent with the **individuals'** needs, their objectives and preferred learning styles

b) the **support** you provide takes account of the **individuals'** work constraints and overall team objectives

c) you give all team members equal access to **support** relevant to their learning needs

d) you monitor the **individuals'** learning and development carefully so that you can modify **support** promptly, according to their needs

e) you encourage, collect and respond constructively to feedback from **individuals** on the quality of **support** you provide

f) you give feedback to **individuals** at points most likely to reinforce learning and development

g) the feedback you give is accurate, objective and helpful

h) you identify and remove any obstacles to learning effectively and with the agreement of the **individuals** involved.

Knowledge requirements

You need to know and understand

Equal opportunities

- the importance of equality of opportunity in implementing development activities and how to ensure this.

Monitoring and evaluation

- the importance of monitoring individual progress
- how to monitor and evaluate individual progress and make adjustments according to a range of factors which you identify
- the importance of gathering feedback on the quality of support you provide
- how to encourage and enable the individuals you support to provide useful feedback
- the importance of providing accurate, objective and constructive feedback to individuals on their progress
- how to provide feedback according to the individual and the circumstances.

Providing support

- the importance of managers supporting individual learning and development
- the types of support for individual learning and development which your team members may need
- the importance of ensuring that methods of support fit the individuals' needs, objectives and preferred learning styles
- how to choose methods of support which are appropriate to individuals' needs
- the range of obstacles to learning and development which individuals may encounter, how to identify these and strategies to use in response to them.

Evidence requirements

You must prove that you *support individual learning and development* to the National Standard of competence.

To do this, you must provide evidence to convince your assessor that you consistently meet **all** the performance criteria.

Your evidence must be the result of real work activities undertaken by yourself. Evidence from simulated activities is **only** acceptable for performance criterion h) in this element.

You must show evidence that you provide at least **two** of the following types of **support**

- mentoring
- coaching
- provision of learning opportunities at work.

You must also show evidence that you support at least **one** of the following types of **individuals**

- team members
- colleagues working at the same level as yourself
- people working in another team whom you have been asked to support
- people working temporarily in your organisation.

You must, however, convince your assessor that you have the necessary knowledge, understanding and skills to be able to perform competently in respect of **all** types of **support** and **individuals**, listed above.

Develop teams and individuals
to enhance performance

Assess the development of teams and individuals

Performance criteria

You must ensure that

a) you agree the **purpose** of the **assessment** and your own role in it with relevant people

b) you give opportunities to team members to contribute to their own and their team's **assessments**

c) you give all team members equal access to **assessment** against development objectives

d) you carry out the **assessments** objectively against clear, agreed criteria

e) you base the **assessments** on sufficient, valid and reliable information

f) you provide information on the results of the **assessments** to authorised people only, in an appropriate format and to agreed deadlines.

Knowledge requirements

You need to know and understand

Equal opportunities
- the importance of equality of opportunity in providing opportunities for teams and individuals to contribute to their own assessments and how to ensure this.

Information handling
- how to collect and validate the information you need
- the importance of confidentiality when carrying out and reporting assessments.

Involvement and motivation
- the importance of agreeing the purpose of the assessments with relevant people
- the importance of team members contributing to the assessment of their own progress and how to encourage and enable them to do so.

Organisational context
- procedures for reporting the results of assessment.

Training and development
- the importance of assessing team members against development activities
- the team's development objectives
- the range of purposes which assessments have
- the principles of fair and objective assessment
- the methods which may be used to assess the development of team members
- the information required to assess team members' development.

Evidence requirements

You must prove that you *assess the development of teams and individuals* to the National Standard of competence.

To do this, you must provide evidence to convince your assessor that you consistently meet **all** the performance criteria.

Your evidence must be the result of real work activities undertaken by yourself. Evidence from simulated activities is **not** acceptable for this element.

You must show evidence that you carry out assessments with at least **two** of the following types of **purpose**
- to identify further development needs
- to evaluate the effectiveness of development processes
- to appraise performance
- to recognise knowledge, skills and competence at work.

You must also show evidence that you carry out at least **two** of the following types of **assessment**
- testing of knowledge and skills
- observing performance at work
- assessing the contributions of colleagues and team members
- taking part in appraisal discussions.

You must, however, convince your assessor that you have the necessary knowledge, understanding and skills to be able to perform competently in respect of **all** types of **purpose** and **assessment**, listed above.

Develop teams and individuals
to enhance performance

Element C10.6

Improve the development of teams and individuals

Performance criteria

You must ensure that

a) you give opportunities to those involved to help evaluate and improve **development activities**

b) your evaluation of the usefulness and applicability of **development activities** is based on sufficient valid and relevant information

c) your evaluation demonstrates the contribution **development activities** make to achieving team and organisational objectives

d) where **development activities** prove ineffective or inappropriate, you agree alternatives which are capable of meeting the development needs you have identified

e) you present your recommendations for improving overall development practice to **relevant people** in an appropriate and timely manner.

Knowledge requirements

You need to know and understand

Communication

- how to present recommendations in a way which is likely to influence decision-makers positively.

Continuous improvement

- the importance of continually reviewing and improving development activities to ongoing organisational effectiveness
- how to evaluate the contribution which development activities make to achieving team and organisational objectives and identify better alternatives
- the information which is needed to evaluate the usefulness and applicability of development activities.

Information handling

- how to collect and check the validity of the information you need.

Involvement and motivation

- the importance of giving opportunities to those involved to contribute to the evaluation and improvement of development activities
- how to encourage and enable those involved to provide useful feedback.

Organisational context

- procedures to follow when making recommendations to improve development activities.

Evidence requirements

You must prove that you *improve the development of teams and individuals* to the National Standard of competence.

To do this, you must provide evidence to convince your assessor that you consistently meet **all** the performance criteria.

Your evidence must be the result of real work activities undertaken by yourself. Evidence from simulated activities is **not** acceptable for this element.

You must show evidence that you evaluate and improve at least **two** of the following types of **development activities**

- naturally occurring learning opportunities at work
- specifically designed learning opportunities at work
- formal training
- informal training.

You must also show evidence that you pass on your recommendations to at least **two** of the following types of **relevant people**

- team members
- colleagues working at the same level as yourself
- higher-level managers or sponsors
- specialists.

You must, however, convince your assessor that you have the necessary knowledge, understanding and skills to be able to perform competently in respect of **all** types of **development activities** and **relevant people**, listed above.

Manage the performance of teams and individuals

Unit summary

This unit is about making the best use of your team and its members so that they can achieve your organisation's objectives. It covers allocating work, agreeing objectives, and setting out plans and methods of working. It also involves monitoring and evaluating the work of your team and its members and providing feedback to them on their performance.

This unit contains four elements

C13.1 *Allocate work to teams and individuals*
C13.2 *Agree objectives and work plans with teams and individuals*
C13.3 *Assess the performance of teams and individuals*
C13.4 *Provide feedback to teams and individuals on their performance.*

Personal competencies

In performing effectively in this unit, you will show that you

Acting assertively
- take a leading role in initiating action and making decisions
- take personal responsibility for making things happen
- take control of situations and events

Building teams
- actively build relationships with others
- make time available to support others
- encourage and stimulate others to make the best use of their abilities
- evaluate and enhance people's capability to do their jobs
- provide feedback designed to improve people's future performance
- show respect for the views and actions of others
- show sensitivity to the needs and feelings of others
- use power and authority in a fair and equitable manner
- keep others informed about plans and progress
- clearly identify what is required of others
- invite others to contribute to planning and organising work
- set objectives which are both achievable and challenging
- check individuals' commitment to a specific course of action
- use a variety of techniques to promote morale and productivity
- identify and resolve causes of conflict or resistance

Communicating
- listen actively, ask questions, clarify points and rephrase others' statements and check mutual understanding
- adopt communication styles appropriate to listeners and situations, including selecting an appropriate time and place
- confirm listeners' understanding through questioning and interpretation of non-verbal signals
- modify communication in response to feedback from listeners

Thinking and taking decisions
- break processes down into tasks and activities
- take decisions which are realistic for the situation.

Manage the performance of teams and individuals

Allocate work to teams and individuals

Performance criteria

You must ensure that

a) you give opportunities to your team members to recommend how you should **allocate** work within the team

b) your **allocation** of work makes the best use of your team's resources and the abilities of all its members

c) your **allocation** of work provides your team members with suitable learning opportunities to meet their personal development objectives

d) your **allocation** of work is consistent with your team's objectives, and the objectives, policies and values of your organisation

e) you clearly define the responsibilities of your team and its individual members, and the limits of their authority

f) you provide sufficient **information** on your **allocation** of work in a manner and at a level and pace appropriate to the individuals concerned

g) you confirm team and individual understanding of, and commitment to, work **allocations** at appropriate intervals

h) where team resources are insufficient, you reach agreement with **relevant people** on the prioritisation of objectives or reallocation of resources

i) you inform your team and its members of changes to work **allocations** in a way which minimises the impact on time, cost and inconvenience.

Knowledge requirements

You need to know and understand

Communication

- the importance of defining and communicating team and individual responsibilities clearly
- how to communicate team and individual responsibilities clearly to those involved
- how to develop and present work plans using spoken, written and graphical means.

Delegation

- the importance of the effective allocation of work to your team's performance and your role and responsibilities in relation to this
- the factors which you need to consider when allocating work to individuals within the team
- how to match the allocation of work to learning needs and individual development plans
- how to prioritise and re-prioritise work allocations according to resource availability
- how your changes to work allocations and negotiations around them can impact on cost, time and convenience.

Involvement and motivation

- why your team members should have the opportunity to recommend work allocations
- how to encourage and enable team members to provide suggestions on the allocation of work and be committed to their responsibilities.

Organisational context

- your team objectives, and the organisational policies and values which have a bearing on the allocation of work within your team
- the relevant people with whom negotiations on the allocation of resources need to take place

Evidence requirements

You must prove that you *allocate work to teams and individuals* to the National Standard of competence.

To do this, you must provide evidence to convince your assessor that you consistently meet **all** the performance criteria.

Your evidence must be the result of real work activities undertaken by yourself. Evidence from simulated activities is **only** acceptable for performance criterion h) in this element.

You must show evidence that you make **allocations** covering **both** of the following contexts

- normal working
- emergencies.

You must show evidence that you provide at least **two** of the following types of **information**

- spoken
- written
- graphical.

You must also show evidence that you reach agreement with at least **two** of the following types of **relevant people**

- team members
- colleagues working at the same level as yourself
- higher-level managers or sponsors
- customers
- suppliers.

You must, however, convince your assessor that you have the necessary knowledge, understanding and skills to be able to perform competently in respect of **all** types of **information** and **relevant people**, listed above.

**Manage the performance of
teams and individuals**

Element C13.2

Agree objectives and work plans with teams and individuals

Performance criteria

You must ensure that

a) you give opportunities to your **team members** to help define their own **objectives and work plans**

b) you develop **objectives and work plans** which are consistent with team and organisational objectives and agree these with all personnel in your area of responsibility

c) the **objectives, work plans** and schedules are realistic and achievable within **organisational constraints**

d) the **objectives and work plans** take account of **team members'** abilities and development needs

e) you explain the **objectives and work plans** in sufficient detail and at a level and pace appropriate to your individual **team members**

f) you confirm team and individual understanding of, and commitment to, **objectives and work plans** at appropriate intervals

g) you provide advice and guidance on how to achieve **objectives** in sufficient detail and at times appropriate to the needs of teams and individuals

h) you update the **objectives and work plans** regularly and take account of any individual, team and organisational changes.

Knowledge requirements

You need to know and understand

Communication
- the importance of good communication when explaining objectives and work plans.

Involvement and motivation
- the importance of consulting with team members and achieving consensus and agreement on objectives and work plans
- how to encourage and enable team members to define their own work objectives and plans
- how to gain the commitment of team members to objectives and work plans
- the types of issues on which your team members may need advice and guidance.

Organisational context
- the organisational objectives and constraints which have a bearing on objectives and work plans.

Planning
- how to identify and devise objectives and work plans for the short, medium and long term
- the importance of agreeing objectives and work plans which are realistic and achievable
- how to match objectives and work plans with individuals' abilities and development needs
- the importance of regularly updating objectives and work plans
- the difference between someone who is within the manager's line management control and someone for whom the manager has functional responsibility, and the implications this difference may have for planning work.

Evidence requirements

You must prove that you *agree objectives and work plans with teams and individuals* to the National Standard of competence.

To do this, you must provide evidence to convince your assessor that you consistently meet **all** the performance criteria.

Your evidence must be the result of real work activities undertaken by yourself. Evidence from simulated activities is **not** acceptable for this element.

You must show evidence that you involve and plan work with at least **one** of the following types of **team member**
- people for whom you have line responsibility
- people for whom you have functional responsibility.

You must show evidence that you agree at least **two** of the following types of **objectives and work plans**
- short-term
- medium-term
- long-term.

You must also show evidence that you take account of **all** of the following types of **organisational constraints**
- organisational objectives
- organisational policies
- resources.

You must, however, convince your assessor that you have the necessary knowledge, understanding and skills to be able to perform competently in respect of **all** types of **team member** and **objectives and work plans**, listed above.

Manage the performance of
teams and individuals

Element C13.3

Assess the performance of teams and individuals

Performance criteria

You must ensure that

a) you clearly explain the **purpose** of **monitoring and assessment** to all those involved

b) you give opportunities to teams and individuals to **monitor and assess** their own performance against objectives and work plans

c) you **monitor** the performance of teams and individuals at times most likely to maintain and improve effective performance

d) your **assessment** of the performance of teams and individuals is based on sufficient, valid and reliable **information**

e) you carry out your **assessments** objectively, against clear, agreed criteria

f) your **assessments** take due account of the personal circumstances of team members and the **organisational constraints** on their work.

Knowledge requirements

You need to know and understand

Communication

- the importance of being clear yourself about the purpose of monitoring and assessment and communicating this effectively to those involved.

Continuous improvement

- the importance of monitoring and assessing the ongoing performance of teams and individuals
- different purposes of work monitoring and assessment
- how to make fair and objective assessments
- how to monitor and assess the performance of teams and individuals
- the standards against which work is to be assessed
- the information needed to assess the performance of teams and individuals.

Information handling

- how the necessary information should be gathered and validated.

Involvement and motivation

- the importance of providing opportunities to team members to monitor and assess their own work, and how to enable this.

Organisational context

- the organisational constraints which may affect the achievement of objectives.

Providing support

- the types of personal circumstances which may impact on individual performance.

Evidence requirements

You must prove that you *assess the performance of teams and individuals* to the National Standard of competence.

To do this, you must provide evidence to convince your assessor that you consistently meet **all** the performance criteria.

Your evidence must be the result of real work activities undertaken by yourself. Evidence from simulated activities is **not** acceptable for this element.

You must show evidence that your assessments have at least **two** of the following types of **purpose**

- assuring that objectives have been achieved
- assuring that quality and customer requirements have been met
- appraising team or individual performance
- assessing performance for reward
- recognising competent performance and achievement.

You must show evidence that you use at least **one** of the following types of **monitoring and assessment**

- specific to one activity or objective
- general to overall performance of the team or individual.

You must show evidence that you use **both** of the following types of **information**

- qualitative
- quantitative.

You must also show evidence that you take account of **all** the following types of **organisational constraints**

- organisational objectives
- organisational policies
- resources.

You must, however, convince your assessor that you have the necessary knowledge, understanding and skills to be able to perform competently in respect of **all** types of **purpose** and **monitoring and assessment**, listed above.

Manage the performance of teams and individuals

Element C13.4

Provide feedback to teams and individuals on their performance

Performance criteria

You must ensure that

a) you provide **feedback** to teams and individuals in a **situation** and in a **form** and manner most likely to maintain and improve their performance

b) the **feedback** you provide is clear, and is based on your objective assessment of their performance against agreed objectives

c) your **feedback** acknowledges your team members' achievement

d) your **feedback** provides your team members with constructive suggestions and encouragement for improving future performance against their work and development objectives

e) the way in which you provide **feedback** shows respect for individuals and the need for confidentiality

f) you give opportunities to teams and individuals to respond to **feedback,** and to recommend how they could improve their performance in the future.

Knowledge requirements

You need to know and understand

Communication
- the importance of good communication skills when providing feedback
- how to provide both positive and negative feedback to team members on their performance
- how to choose an appropriate time and place to give feedback to teams and individuals
- how to provide feedback in a way which encourages your team members to feel that you respect them

Continuous improvement
- the importance of providing clear and accurate feedback to your team members on their performance and your role and responsibilities in relation to this.

Information handling
- the principles of confidentiality when providing feedback – which people should receive which pieces of information.

Involvement and motivation
- how to motivate team members and gain their commitment by providing feedback
- the importance of being encouraging when providing feedback to team members and showing respect for those involved
- the importance of providing constructive suggestions on how performance can be improved
- the importance of giving those involved the opportunity to provide suggestions on how to improve their work.

Evidence requirements

You must prove that you *provide feedback to teams and individuals on their performance* to the National Standard of competence.

To do this, you must provide evidence to convince your assessor that you consistently meet **all** the performance criteria.

Your evidence must be the result of real work activities undertaken by yourself. Evidence from simulated activities is **not** acceptable for this element.

You must show evidence that you provide **both** of the following types of **feedback**
- positive
- negative.

You must show evidence that you use **both** of the following **forms** of feedback
- spoken
- written.

You must also show evidence that you give feedback in at least **three** of the following types of **situation**
- during normal day-to-day activities
- when required to maintain motivation, morale and effectiveness
- during formal appraisals
- at team meetings and briefings
- during confidential discussions of work.

You must, however, convince your assessor that you have the necessary knowledge, understanding and skills to be able to perform competently in respect of **all** types of **situation**, listed above.

Deal with poor performance in your team

Unit summary

This unit is about dealing with team members whose performance is unsatisfactory. It covers identifying their problems and providing support to help them deal with these. It covers contributing to disciplinary and grievance procedures when work is consistently below standard or if a team member has a serious complaint against your organisation or someone in it. It also covers dismissing team members if their performance or conduct means that no other course of action is acceptable.

This unit contains three elements

C16.1 *Support team members who have problems affecting their performance*
C16.2 *Implement disciplinary and grievance procedures*
C16.3 *Dismiss team members whose performance is unsatisfactory.*

Personal competencies

In performing effectively in this unit, you will show that you

Acting assertively
- act in an assured and unhesitating manner when faced with a challenge
- state your own position and views clearly in conflict situations
- maintain your beliefs, commitment and effort in spite of set-backs or opposition

Behaving ethically
- comply with legislation, industry regulation, professional and organisational codes
- show integrity and fairness in decision-making

Building teams
- make time available to support others
- encourage and stimulate others to make the best use of their abilities
- show respect for the views and actions of others
- show sensitivity to the needs and feelings of others
- use power and authority in a fair and equitable manner
- clearly identify what is required of others
- check individuals' commitment to a specific course of action
- use a variety of techniques to promote morale and productivity
- identify and resolve causes of conflict or resistance

Communicating
- listen actively, ask questions, clarify points and rephrase others' statements to check mutual understanding
- confirm listeners' understanding through questioning and interpretation of non-verbal signals
- encourage listeners to ask questions or rephrase statements to clarify their understanding
- modify communication in response to feedback from listeners

Focusing on results
- maintain a focus on objectives
- establish and communicate high expectations of performance, including setting an example to others
- monitor quality of work and progress against plans
- continually strive to identify and minimise barriers to excellence.

Deal with poor performance in your team

Element C16.1

Support team members who have problems affecting their performance

Performance criteria

You must ensure that

a) you promptly identify poor performance and bring it directly to the attention of the **team member** concerned

b) you give the **team member** the opportunity to discuss actual or potential **problems** affecting their performance

c) you discuss these issues with the **team member** at a time and place appropriate to the type, seriousness and complexity of the **problem**

d) you gather and check as much information as possible to identify the nature of the **problem**

e) you agree with the **team member** a course of action which is appropriate, timely and effective

f) where necessary, you refer the **team member** to support services appropriate to their individual circumstances

g) the way you respond to **team members' problems** maintains respect for the individual and the need for confidentiality

h) you plan and agree follow-up action with the **team member** concerned, to ensure positive outcomes

i) you promptly inform relevant people of **problems** beyond your level of responsibility or competence.

Knowledge requirements

You need to know and understand

Communication
- the importance of providing opportunities for team members to discuss problems
- how to encourage and enable team members to talk frankly about their problems.

Information handling
- the importance of confidentiality.

Monitoring and evaluation
- the importance of promptly identifying poor performance and bringing it directly to team members' attention.

Providing support
- your role and responsibilities in dealing with team members' problems
- the types of problems which your team members may encounter at work
- how to identify problems which the individual is experiencing and devise appropriate responses
- the importance of agreeing a course of action with the team member and following this up
- how to decide when the problem goes beyond your own level of competence and responsibility
- the range of support services which exist inside and outside your organisation.

Working relationships
- the importance of maintaining respect for the individual
- the limits beyond which you should not go in becoming involved in the individual's problem.

Evidence requirements

You must prove that you *support team members who have problems affecting their performance* to the National Standard of competence.

To do this, you must provide evidence to convince your assessor that you consistently meet **all** the performance criteria.

Your evidence must be the result of real work activities undertaken by yourself. Evidence from simulated activities is **only** acceptable for performance criterion f) in this element.

You must show evidence that you help at least **one** of the following types of **team members**
- people for whom you have line management responsibility
- people for whom you have functional responsibility.

You must also show evidence that you help team members with at least **one** of the following types of **problems**
- arising from work-related factors
- arising from external personal factors.

You must, however, convince your assessor that you have the necessary knowledge, understanding and skills to be able to perform competently in respect of **all** types of **team members** and **problems**, listed above.

Deal with poor performance in your team

Element C16.2

Implement disciplinary and grievance procedures

Performance criteria

You must ensure that

a) your team members have clear, accurate and timely **information** regarding disciplinary and grievance procedures

b) you implement disciplinary and grievance procedures in a fair, impartial and timely way

c) you implement disciplinary and grievance procedures according to your organisational values and policies, and the relevant legal requirements

d) the way you implement disciplinary and grievance procedures maintains respect for the individual and the need for confidentiality

e) your records of the proceedings and their outcomes are accurate and complete, and you make them available only to authorised people.

Knowledge requirements

You need to know and understand

Disciplinary and grievance procedures
- the importance of effectively applying disciplinary and grievance procedures and your responsibilities in relation to this
- situations in which disciplinary and grievance procedures should be implemented
- the importance of informing team members about disciplinary and grievance procedures, appropriate times to do so and methods to use
- the importance of fairness, impartiality and responding in a timely way when dealing with disciplinary and grievance procedures.

Information handling
- the importance of confidentiality when dealing with disciplinary and grievance procedures—who may receive what information
- the importance of good record-keeping and how to do so.

Legal requirements
- the legal requirements relevant to disciplinary and grievance procedures.

Organisational context
- the organisational values and policies relevant to disciplinary and grievance procedures.

Working relationships
- the importance of maintaining respect for the individual when dealing with disciplinary and grievance procedures.

Evidence requirements

You must prove that you *implement disciplinary and grievance procedures* to the National Standard of competence.

To do this, you must provide evidence to convince your assessor that you consistently meet **all** the performance criteria.

Your evidence should be the result of real work activities undertaken by yourself. However, evidence from simulated activities **is** acceptable for this element.

You must show evidence that you provide **both** of the following types of **information**
- organisational
- legal.

Deal with poor performance in
your team

Element C16.3

Dismiss team members whose performance is unsatisfactory

Performance criteria

You must ensure that

a) the way you dismiss individuals is fair, impartial and takes place at an appropriate time

b) you obtain appropriate advice on dismissal from **relevant people**

c) you give clear **reasons for dismissal** to the individual concerned at a level and pace appropriate to them

d) the process of dismissal complies with the organisation's disciplinary and grievance procedures and legal requirements

e) the process of dismissal maintains respect for the individual and the need for confidentiality

f) you keep accurate records of the dismissal

g) you provide accurate and non-confidential information regarding the dismissal to other team members and colleagues in a way which maintains confidence and morale.

Knowledge requirements

You need to know and understand

Disciplinary and grievance procedures

- your role and responsibilities regarding the dismissal of staff
- the types of situations in which the dismissal of staff is necessary
- the importance of fairness and impartiality when dismissing staff
- the situations in which the advice and support of others may be required – who to contact according to the context
- the importance of giving the reasons for dismissal clearly to the individual concerned and how to do so according to the context, individual and reason for dismissal.

Information handling

- the importance of confidentiality when dealing with disciplinary and grievance procedures
- the importance of good record-keeping.

Involvement and motivation

- the importance of explaining the dismissal and the reasons for dismissal to team members and colleagues.

Legal requirements

- the legal requirements covering the dismissal of staff.

Organisational context

- the organisational requirements and procedures covering the dismissal of staff.

Working relationships

- the importance of maintaining respect for the individual when dismissing staff.

Evidence requirements

You must prove that you *dismiss team members whose performance is unsatisfactory* to the National Standard of competence.

To do this, you must provide evidence to convince your assessor that you consistently meet **all** the performance criteria.

Your evidence should be the result of real work activities undertaken by yourself. However, evidence from simulated activities **is** acceptable for this element.

You must show evidence that you cover **one** of the following types of **reason for dismissal**

- sub-standard work
- gross misconduct.

You must also show evidence that you seek advice from at least **one** of the following types of **relevant people**

- colleagues working at the same level as yourself
- higher-level managers
- specialists.

You must, however, convince your assessor that you have the necessary knowledge, understanding and skills to be able to perform competently in respect of **all** types of **reasons for dismissal** and **relevant people**, listed above.

Redeploy personnel and make redundancies

Unit summary

This unit is about transferring people to other posts and making staff redundant in response to developments or structural changes. It covers planning redeployment, implementing those plans and making personnel redundant.

This unit contains three elements

C17.1 *Plan the redeployment of personnel*
C17.2 *Redeploy personnel*
C17.3 *Make personnel redundant.*

Personal competencies

In performing effectively in this unit, you will show that you

Acting assertively
- act in an assured and unhesitating manner when faced with a challenge
- state your own position and views clearly in conflict situations
- maintain your beliefs, commitment and effort in spite of set-backs or opposition

Acting strategically
- display understanding of how the different parts of the organisation and its environment fit together
- clearly relate your goals and actions to the strategic aims of your organisation
- take opportunities when they arise to achieve the longer-term aims or needs of your organisation

Behaving ethically
- comply with legislation, industry regulation, professional and organisational codes
- show integrity and fairness in decision-making

Building teams
- make time available to support others
- encourage and stimulate others to make the best use of their abilities
- show respect for the views and actions of others
- show sensitivity to the needs and feelings of others
- use power and authority in a fair and equitable manner
- use a variety of techniques to promote morale and productivity
- identify and resolve causes of conflict or resistance

Communicating
- confirm listeners' understanding through questioning and interpretation of non-verbal signals
- encourage listeners to ask questions or rephrase statements to clarify their understanding
- modify communication in response to feedback from listeners

Managing self
- remain calm in difficult or uncertain situations
- handle others' emotions without becoming personally involved in them.

Redeploy personnel and make
redundancies

Element C17.1

Plan the redeployment of personnel

Performance criteria

You must ensure that

a) you provide clear and accurate information on the proposed **redeployment** to **relevant people** at an appropriate time

b) you give opportunities for **relevant people** to comment on the proposed **redeployment** and to contribute to planning its implementation

c) your case for the proposed **redeployment** is clear and supported by sound evidence

d) your plans for **redeployment** are comprehensive, accurate and consistent with your organisational values and objectives

e) your plans for **redeployment** take account of the personal qualities, situation and preferences of those involved

f) your plans for **redeployment** provide equal opportunities for all those suitably qualified to benefit

g) you obtain and provide sufficient resources to meet the costs of **redeployment**

h) the way you discuss your plans for **redeployment** demonstrates respect for individuals involved and the need for confidentiality.

Knowledge requirements

You need to know and understand

Communication
- how to construct and present a case for redeployment in a way which will positively influence decision-making.

Equal opportunities
- the importance of equal opportunities when planning redeployment.

Information handling
- the importance of confidentiality when planning redeployment.

Involvement and motivation
- the importance of consulting on redeployment plans and how to do so.

Legal requirements
- laws covering the redeployment of staff.

Planning
- how to plan for redeployment and ensure that these plans are consistent with the relevant organisational values and objectives
- the importance of taking account of the personal qualities, competences, situation and preferences of those involved and the constraints which affect how much these factors can influence your final plans
- how to estimate the resources needed to support redeployment.

Redeployment and redundancy
- the types of situations in which redeployment may be appropriate and factors which influence decisions on whether redeployment is a feasible option.

Evidence requirements

You must prove that you *plan the redeployment of personnel* to the National Standard of competence.

To do this, you must provide evidence to convince your assessor that you consistently meet **all** the performance criteria.

Your evidence must be the result of real work activities undertaken by yourself. Evidence from simulated activities is **not** acceptable for this element.

You must show evidence that you plan at least **one** of the following types of **redeployment**
- moving team members from one project to another
- moving team members from one part of the organisation to another
- moving team members out of the organisation.

You must also show evidence that you consult with at least **two** of the following types of **relevant people**
- team members
- colleagues working at the same level as yourself
- higher-level managers or sponsors
- specialists
- people outside your organisation.

You must, however, convince your assessor that you have the necessary knowledge, understanding and skills to be able to perform competently in respect of **all** types of **redeployment** and **relevant people**, listed above.

Redeploy personnel and make
redundancies

Element C17.2

Redeploy personnel

Performance criteria

You must ensure that

a) you present your plans for
   redeployment to **relevant people** at
   an appropriate time, level and pace

b) you provide **preparation and support**
   to those being redeployed which is
   sufficient to make them effective in their
   new roles

c) you monitor the **redeployment** in a
   way which allows you to identify
   problems at an early stage

d) you modify your **redeployment** plans
   to resolve any problems you identify

e) the way you carry out **redeployment**
   demonstrates respect for individuals
   and the need for confidentiality.

Knowledge requirements

You need to know and understand

Communication
- how to inform people about your redeployment plans in a way which is appropriate to the situation and those involved.

Information handling
- the importance of confidentiality when carrying out redeployment – who may receive what information.

Involvement and motivation
- the importance of presenting plans for redeployment to team members, colleagues, line managers, specialists and people outside the organisation clearly and at an appropriate time.

Monitoring and evaluation
- the importance of monitoring redeployment
- the types of problems which may arise as a result and how to respond to these.

Providing support
- the types of preparation and support which redeployed personnel may require and how to provide these.

Working relationships
- the importance of maintaining respect for the individual during the process of redeployment
- how to convey the feeling that you respect the individuals involved.

Evidence requirements

You must prove that you *redeploy personnel* to the National Standard of competence.

To do this, you must provide evidence to convince your assessor that you consistently meet **all** the performance criteria.

Your evidence must be the result of real work activities undertaken by yourself. Evidence from simulated activities is **not** acceptable for this element.

You must show evidence that you use at least **one** of the following types of **redeployment**
- moving team members from one project to another
- moving team members from one part of the organisation to another
- moving team members out of the organisation.

You must show evidence that you present your plans to at least **two** of the following types of **relevant people**
- team members
- colleagues working at the same level as yourself
- higher-level managers or sponsors
- specialists
- people outside your organisation.

You must also show evidence that you organise at least **two** of the following types of **preparation and support**
- induction to new role
- training and development in knowledge and skills needed for the new post
- ongoing support from yourself.

You must, however, convince your assessor that you have the necessary knowledge, understanding and skills to be able to perform competently in respect of **all** types of **redeployment**, **relevant people** and **preparation and support**, listed above.

Redeploy personnel and make redundancies

Make personnel redundant

Performance criteria

You must ensure that

a) your team members receive information on redundancy policy, procedures and criteria which is accurate, relevant and sufficient for their needs

b) you agree your redundancy plans with **relevant people**

c) your selection of personnel whose **jobs** are redundant is based on the fair and consistent assessment of relevant information against objective criteria

d) the way you carry out the redundancy process is consistent with organisational and legal requirements

e) the information you provide to personnel whose **jobs** are redundant is clear, accurate and meets organisational and legal requirements

f) where appropriate, you provide alternative suitable employment opportunities and counselling

g) the information you provide to **relevant people** about the redundancy process is accurate, non-confidential and necessary to maintain confidence and morale

h) you make recommendations for improvements to redundancy policy and procedures to **relevant people** in a suitable format.

Knowledge requirements

You need to know and understand

Communication
- the importance of providing clear and accurate information on redundancy policy and procedures to team members.

Involvement and motivation
- the importance of agreeing plans with relevant people
- the importance of maintaining confidence and morale in redundancy situations and strategies to achieve this.

Providing support
- the sources of counselling which may be available.

Redeployment and redundancy
- the relative advantages and disadvantages of redundancy compared to other possible strategies
- how to carry out cost benefit analyses to support decisions about redundancy
- legal and organisational requirements and procedures regarding redundancy
- the information needed when making decisions about redundancy
- the importance of fairness and consistency when assessing the suitability of personnel for redundancy
- the information which you should provide to the personnel being made redundant
- how to identify, select and recommend alternative employment opportunities
- procedures to follow when recommending improvements to redundancy arrangements.

Evidence requirements

You must prove that you *make personnel redundant* to the National Standard of competence.

To do this, you must provide evidence to convince your assessor that you consistently meet **all** the performance criteria.

Your evidence should be the result of real work activities undertaken by yourself. However, evidence from simulated activities **is** acceptable for this element.

You must show evidence that you make redundant people with **jobs** which are
- permanent

You must also show evidence that you consult with and make recommendations to at least **two** of the following types of **relevant people**
- team members
- colleagues working at the same level as yourself
- higher-level managers or sponsors
- specialists
- people outside your organisation.

You must, however, convince your assessor that you have the necessary knowledge, understanding and skills to be able to perform competently in respect of **all** types of **relevant people** listed above and in respect of temporary **jobs**.

Chair and participate in meetings

Unit summary

This unit is about chairing and contributing to meetings so that the objectives of the meetings can be achieved.

This unit contains two elements

D3.1 *Chair meetings*
D3.2 *Participate in meetings.*

Personal competencies

In performing effectively in this unit, you will show that you

Acting assertively
- take a leading role in initiating action and making decisions
- act in an assured and unhesitating manner when faced with a challenge
- say no to unreasonable requests
- maintain your beliefs, commitment and effort in spite of set-backs or opposition

Building teams
- actively build relationships with others
- show respect for the views and actions of others
- show sensitivity to the needs and feelings of others
- use power and authority in a fair and equitable manner
- invite others to contribute to planning and organising work

Communicating
- listen actively, ask questions, clarify points and rephrase others' statements to check mutual understanding
- identify the information needs of listeners
- adopt communication styles appropriate to listeners and situations, including selecting an appropriate time and place
- confirm listeners' understanding through questioning and interpretation of non-verbal signals
- encourage listeners to ask questions or rephrase statements to clarify their understanding
- modify communication in response to feedback from listeners

Focusing on results
- prioritise objectives and schedule work to make best use of time and resources

Influencing others
- present yourself positively to others
- use a variety of means to influence others

Searching for information
- actively encourage the free exchange of information
- push for concrete information in an ambiguous situation

Thinking and taking decisions
- produce a variety of solutions before taking a decision
- reconcile and make use of a variety of perspectives when making sense of a situation
- produce your own ideas from experience and practice
- take decisions which are realistic for the situation
- take decisions in uncertain situations or based on restricted information when necessary.

Chair and participate in meetings

Element D3.1

Chair meetings

Performance criteria

You must ensure that

a) you give people, appropriate to the **purpose** of the **meeting**, sufficient notice and information to allow them to contribute effectively

b) everyone attending the **meeting** agrees the objectives of the **meeting** at the start

c) you allocate discussion time to topics in a way which is consistent with their importance, urgency and complexity

d) your style of leadership helps those attending the **meeting** to make useful contributions

e) you discourage unhelpful arguments and digressions

f) you present information and provide summaries clearly, at appropriate points during the **meeting**

g) the **meeting** achieves its objectives within the allocated time

h) agreed decisions and recommendations fall within the group's authority

i) you give clear, accurate and concise information about decisions and recommendations to those who need it

j) you seek feedback from those attending and use this to improve the effectiveness of future **meetings.**

Knowledge requirements

You need to know and understand

Communication
- how to identify unhelpful arguments and digressions, and strategies which may be used to discourage these
- how to present information during meetings
- how to get and use feedback from others

Leadership styles
- styles of leadership which can be used to run meetings and how to choose a style according the nature of the meeting

Meetings
- the value and limitations of meetings as a method of exchanging information and making decisions
- how to determine when meetings are the most effective method of dealing with issues and possible alternatives which may be used
- potential differences between meetings which are internal and those involving people from outside
- the purpose of agendas and how to devise agendas according to the issues, intended outcomes and time available
- the importance of determining the purpose and objectives of meetings and how to do so
- the importance of summarising discussions and decisions during meetings and at what points this is appropriate
- how to manage discussions so that the objectives of the meeting are met within the allocated time
- the importance of ensuring decisions taken are within the authority of the meeting

Organisational context
- how to determine who are the necessary people to attend the meeting
- procedures to follow when calling meetings and preparing for them.

Evidence requirements

You must prove that you *chair meetings* to the National Standard of competence.

To do this, you must provide evidence to convince your assessor that you consistently meet **all** the performance criteria.

Your evidence must be the result of real work activities undertaken by yourself. Evidence from simulated activities is **not** acceptable for this element.

You must show evidence of chairing meetings with **all** of the following types of **purpose**
- information giving
- consultation
- decision making.

You must also show evidence of chairing **both** of the following types of **meeting**
- involving people from within your organisation
- involving people outside your organisation.

Chair and participate in meetings

Element D3.2

Participate in meetings

Performance criteria

You must ensure that

a) your preparation for the **meeting** is sufficient to enable you to participate effectively

b) you consult with the **people** you are representing sufficiently to allow you to present their views effectively

c) your contributions to the **meeting** are clear, concise and relevant

d) your contributions to the **meeting** help to clarify problems and identify and assess possible solutions

e) you acknowledge and discuss the contributions and viewpoints of others in a constructive manner

f) you give clear, accurate and concise information about decisions made at the **meeting**, promptly to those who need it.

Knowledge requirements

You need to know and understand

Communication

- the information concerning the decisions and recommendations of the meeting which need to be conveyed to others and how to ensure that this has been done effectively

Meetings

- how to prepare for meetings according to different roles and responsibilities which you may have in relation to the meeting
- the importance of consulting in advance with those you are representing and how to do so
- the importance of making clear, concise and relevant contributions to meetings and how to ensure your contributions meet these criteria
- how to identify and analyse the problems discussed in meetings and make contributions capable of clarifying and resolving these

Working relationships

- the importance of constructively acknowledging the contributions and viewpoints of others and how to do so.

Evidence requirements

You must prove that you *participate in meetings* to the National Standard of competence.

To do this, you must provide evidence to convince your assessor that you consistently meet **all** the performance criteria.

Your evidence must be the result of real work activities undertaken by yourself. Evidence from simulated activities is **not** acceptable for this element.

You must also show evidence of contributing to **both** of the following types of **meetings**

- involving people from within your organisation
- involving people outside your organisation.

You must show evidence of representing **both** of the following types of **people**

- individuals
- groups.

Establish information management and communication systems

Unit summary

This unit is about setting up effective communications and information management systems in your organisation. This involves identifying the information and communication needs of your organisation, selecting information management and communications systems which meet those needs, setting these systems up and finally monitoring these systems to ensure their effectiveness.

This unit contains four elements

D5.1 *Identify information and communication requirements*
D5.2 *Select information management and communication systems*
D5.3 *Implement information management and communication systems*
D5.4 *Monitor information management and communication systems.*

Personal competencies

In performing effectively in this unit, you will show that you

Acting strategically
- understand how the different parts of the organisation and its environment fit together
- work towards a clearly defined vision of the future
- clearly relate your goals and actions to the strategic aims of your organisation
- take opportunities when they arise to achieve the longer-term aims or needs of your organisation

Communicating
- listen actively, ask questions, clarify points and rephrase others' statements and check mutual understanding
- adopt communication styles appropriate to listeners and situations, including selecting an appropriate time and place

Influencing others
- present yourself positively to others
- create and prepare strategies for influencing others
- understand the culture of your organisation and act to work within it or influence it

Searching for information
- establish information networks to search for and gather relevant information
- make best use of existing sources of information
- seek information from multiple sources

Thinking and taking decisions
- break processes down into tasks and activities
- use your own experience and evidence from others to identify problems and understand situations
- identify patterns or meaning from events and data which are not obviously related
- produce a variety of solutions before taking a decision
- produce your own ideas from experience and practice
- take decisions which are realistic for the situation.

Establish information management and communication systems

Element D5.1

Identify information and communication requirements

Performance criteria

You must ensure that

a) the research you carry out is sufficient to identify the **information requirements** of **users**

b) the research you carry out is sufficient to identify likely future information flows and communication processes

c) the **information requirements** you specify are clear, accurate and agreed with **users**

d) you identify the resources needed to meet **information requirements**

e) the **information requirements** you specify are consistent with organisational objectives, policies and resource constraints.

Knowledge requirements

You need to know and understand

Agreements and contracts
- the importance of agreeing information requirements with users and how to achieve such agreements

Analytical techniques
- how to analyse and specify information needs

Information handling
- the importance of information systems to the work of organisations and your role and responsibilities in relation to these
- the range of information requirements people may have
- how to identify information requirements
- the likely future flow of information and communication processes
- how to select a method of identifying information, needs according to the users, the situation and organisational and resource constraints

Legal requirements
- legislation governing the collection, storage and dissemination of information

Organisational context
- organisational objectives, policies and resource constraints which have a bearing on specifying information requirements and how to interpret these

Resource management
- how to identify resources which will be required to meet these information requirements.

Evidence requirements

You must prove that you *identify information and communication requirements* to the National Standard of competence.

To do this, you must provide evidence to convince your assessor that you consistently meet **all** the performance criteria.

Your evidence must be the result of real work activities undertaken by yourself. Evidence from simulated activities is **not** acceptable for this element.

You must show evidence that you identify the requirements of at least **two** of the following types of **users**
- team members
- colleagues working at the same level as yourself
- higher-level managers or sponsors
- people outside your organisation.

You must also show evidence that you identify **all** of the following features of **information requirements**
- scope and depth
- purpose to which the information will be put
- format
- accessibility
- communication process
- legal and statutory requirements
- confidentiality requirements.

You must, however, convince your assessor that you have the necessary knowledge, understanding and skills to be able to perform competently in respect of **all** types of **users** listed above.

Establish information management and communication systems

Element D5.2

Select information management and communication systems

Performance criteria

You must ensure that

a) you agree clear criteria for selection of **information management and communication systems** with **users and others involved or affected**

b) you evaluate possible **systems** and identify those which are capable of meeting **user** requirements and organisational objectives within resource constraints

c) your evaluation of potential **systems** accurately identifies their respective benefits and disadvantages

d) the **systems** you propose most closely meet the agreed criteria and comply with organisational policies and legal requirements

e) your proposals include an implementation plan which is agreed with **users and others involved or affected**.

Knowledge requirements

You need to know and understand

Agreements and contracts
- the importance of reaching agreement with people on criteria for systems and how to achieve such agreements

Information handling
- the range of information management and communication systems which may be appropriate and their relative advantages and disadvantages
- how to determine the criteria for selection of information management and communication systems
- how to evaluate possible systems to ensure they meet user requirements and organisational objectives, legal requirements and resource constraints

Legal requirements
- legislation governing the collection, storage and dissemination of information

Planning
- how to develop implementation plans and agree these with users and others involved

Resource management
- how to carry out cost-benefit analyses of information management and communication systems.

Evidence requirements

You must prove that you *select information management and communication systems* to the National Standard of competence.

To do this, you must provide evidence to convince your assessor that you consistently meet **all** the performance criteria.

Your evidence must be the result of real work activities undertaken by yourself. Evidence from simulated activities is **not** acceptable for this element.

You must show evidence that you select **one** of the following types of **information management and communication systems**
- computer based
- non-computer based.

You must also show evidence that you work with **two** of the following types of **users and others involved or affected**
- team members
- colleagues working at the same level as you
- higher-level managers or sponsors
- people outside your organisation.

You must, however, convince your assessor that you have the necessary knowledge, understanding and skills to be able to perform competently in respect of **all** types of **information management and communication systems**, and **users and others involved or affected** listed above.

Establish information management and communication systems

Element D5.3

Implement information management and communication systems

Performance criteria

You must ensure that

a) you present your plans for implementing **information management and communication systems** to **users and others involved or affected** at an appropriate time, level and pace

b) you confirm **users'** understanding of the **system** and their role in its implementation

c) the resources you select are sufficient for the implementation to take place within agreed timescales

d) you monitor the implementation of the **system** at appropriate times against agreed plans

e) you modify implementation activities, as appropriate to resolve any problems arising

f) the way in which you implement **systems** enables **users and others involved and affected** to make effective contributions

g) you implement **information management and communication systems** within the agreed budget and timescales.

Knowledge requirements

You need to know and understand

Communication
- the importance of checking users' understanding of the system and confirming their role in implementing it

Continuous improvement
- how to monitor the implementation of systems
- the types of problems which may arise during implementation and how to overcome these problems

Involvement and motivation
- the importance of consulting on implementation plans and different methods of doing so appropriate to different types of system and user
- the importance of providing opportunities for those involved in the system to make effective contributions to implementation and how to encourage and enable such contributions

Planning
- how to prepare plans for the implementation of information management and communication systems
- factors which influence the development of such plans

Resource management
- how to estimate resources and time needed to implement different types of information management and communication systems.

Evidence requirements

You must prove that you *implement information management and communication systems* to the National Standard of competence.

To do this, you must provide evidence to convince your assessor that you consistently meet **all** the performance criteria.

Your evidence must be the result of real work activities undertaken by yourself. Evidence from simulated activities is **not** acceptable for this element.

You must show evidence that you implement **one** of the following types of **information management and communication systems**
- computer based
- non-computer based.

You must also show evidence that you work with **two** of the following types of **users and others involved or affected**
- team members
- colleagues working at the same level as you
- higher-level managers or sponsors
- people outside your organisation.

You must, however, convince your assessor that you have the necessary knowledge, understanding and skills to be able to perform competently in respect of **all** types of **information management and communication systems,** and **users and others involved or affected** listed above.

**Establish information
management and
communication systems**

Element D5.4

Monitor information management and communication systems

Performance criteria

You must ensure that

a) you continuously provide opportunities for **users** to give feedback on the effectiveness of information management and communication systems

b) your monitoring and **evaluation** of systems take place at appropriate times against agreed criteria

c) your **evaluations** take account of **trends and developments** and likely future requirements

d) you present the results of **evaluations** to **users and others involved or affected** in a manner likely to attract their support for **improvements**

e) you modify information management and communication systems to overcome any problems effectively.

Knowledge requirements

You need to know and understand

Continuous improvement
- the types of problems which may occur in information management and communication systems and how to overcome these

Involvement and motivation
- the importance of continuously providing opportunities to users to give feedback on the effectiveness of systems and how to enable and encourage such feedback
- how to present evaluations to users and others involved or affected in a manner likely to attract their commitment and support to improvements

Monitoring and evaluation
- the importance of monitoring information management systems and your role and responsibilities in relation to this
- how to select and use monitoring and evaluation methods appropriate to the system, context and requirements

Planning
- how to forecast trends and developments inside and outside the organisation which may lead to new requirements.

Evidence requirements

You must prove that you *monitor information management and communication systems* to the National Standard of competence.

To do this, you must provide evidence to convince your assessor that you consistently meet **all** the performance criteria.

Your evidence must be the result of real work activities undertaken by yourself. Evidence from simulated activities is **not** acceptable for this element.

You must show evidence that you work with **three** of the following types of **users and others involved or affected**
- team members
- colleagues working at the same level as you
- higher-level managers or sponsors
- people outside your organisation.

You must show evidence that you use **both** of the following types of **evaluations**
- qualitative
- quantitative.

You must show evidence that you identify **both** of the following types of **trends and developments**
- external
- internal.

You must also show evidence that you make **both** of the following types of **improvements**
- system design
- usage of system.

You must, however, convince your assessor that you have the necessary knowledge, understanding and skills to be able to perform competently in respect of **all** types of **users and others involved or affected** listed above.

Identify the scope for improvement in the way the organisation manages energy

Unit summary

This unit is about evaluating how the organisation manages energy and suggesting possible areas for improvement.

This unit contains two elements

E1.1 *Audit the organisation's performance in the way it manages energy*
E1.2 *Identify improvements to the way the organisation manages energy.*

Personal competencies

In performing effectively in this unit, you will show that you

Acting strategically
- display an understanding of how the different parts of the organisation and its environment fit together
- clearly relate goals and actions to the strategic aims of the organisation

Communicating
- listen actively, ask questions, clarify points and rephrase others' statements to check mutual understanding
- identify the information needs of listeners
- adopt communication styles appropriate to listeners and situations, including selecting an appropriate time and place
- use a variety of media and communication aids to reinforce points and maintain interest
- confirm listeners' understanding through questioning and interpretation of non-verbal signals
- encourage listeners to ask questions or rephrase statements to clarify their understanding
- modify communication in response to feedback from listeners

Influencing others
- develop and use contacts to trade information, and obtain support and resources
- present yourself positively to others
- create and prepare strategies for influencing others
- use a variety of means to influence others
- understand the culture of your organisation and act to work within it or influence it

Searching for information
- establish information networks to search for and gather relevant information
- actively encourage the free exchange of information
- make best use of existing sources of information
- seek information from multiple sources
- challenge the validity and reliability of sources of information.

Identify the scope for improvement in the way the organisation manages energy

Element E1.1

Audit the organisation's performance in the way it manages energy

Performance criteria

You must ensure that

a) you accurately evaluate the impact of the organisation's activities on the use of energy

b) in partnership with **relevant people**, you correctly identify the organisation's energy efficiency initiatives and how they are developed

c) you accurately evaluate how committed the organisation is to its policies on the efficient use of energy

d) you evaluate how well the organisation's energy efficiency initiatives align with its policies and legal requirements

e) you agree with **relevant people** clear, relevant and assessable **performance indicators** for managing energy

f) you present **performance indicators** in formats which meet organisational requirements

g) you accurately measure the organisation's performance against **performance indicators**.

Knowledge requirements

You need to know and understand

Communication
- how to consult and collaborate with relevant people on energy efficiency
- the acceptable formats for presenting performance indicators and how to select formats appropriate to different situations

Energy efficiency
- how the activities of an organisation can affect the energy used
- the range of energy efficiency initiatives available and how they may be developed within organisations

Legal requirements
- the laws which affect the use of energy

Monitoring and evaluation
- how to measure the impact of an organisation's activities on the energy it uses
- how to measure the level of commitment an organisation has to its policies
- how to develop performance indicators for managing energy

Organisational context
- the policies and procedures of the organisation regarding the efficient use of energy.

Evidence requirements

You must prove that you *audit the organisation's performance in the way it manages energy* to the National Standard of competence.

To do this, you must provide evidence to convince your assessor that you consistently meet **all** the performance criteria.

Your evidence must be the result of real work activities undertaken by yourself. Evidence from simulated activities is **not** acceptable for this element.

You must show evidence that you involve at least **three** of the following types of **relevant people**
- the work force
- colleagues working at the same level
- higher-level managers or sponsors
- technical specialists.

You must also show evidence that you use **all** of the following types of **performance indicators**
- energy usage
- costs
- efficiency.

You must, however, convince your assessor that you have the necessary knowledge, understanding and skills to be able to perform competently in respect of **all** types of **relevant people** listed above.

Identify the scope for
improvement in the way the
organisation manages energy

Element E1.2

Identify improvements to the way the organisation manages energy

Performance criteria

You must ensure that

a) you evaluate the findings of your audit and their implications for how energy is used and managed

b) you evaluate how appropriate and effective current energy sources are for the activities for which they are used

c) you assess potential areas for energy savings in partnership with those involved

d) you evaluate the effects of operational activities on energy usage, efficiency and safety

e) you support your proposals for improving the effectiveness of energy usage with sufficient, valid information

f) you present your proposals for improving the effectiveness of energy usage in a suitable **format**.

Knowledge requirements

You need to know and understand

Communication
- how to consult and collaborate with those involved
- how to develop and present an effective case for improvement

Energy efficiency
- the energy performance indicators and the organisation's current performance against these
- the findings of your energy audit and how to identify their implications for energy usage and management
- the types of energy source available – electricity, gas, oil, solid fuels, nuclear and renewable sources – and their relative appropriateness and effectiveness for different activities
- the principal techniques and technologies which support the efficient use of energy
- how to identify areas where energy savings may be made and how to estimate and assess the potential savings
- how to evaluate the effects of organisational activities on energy usage, efficiency and safety

Health and safety
- the relevant safety legislation, systems and procedures

Information handling
- how to gather information and assess whether it is valid and sufficient

Organisational context
- the policies and procedures of the organisation regarding the efficient use of energy.

Evidence requirements

You must prove that you *identify improvements to the way the organisation manages energy* to the National Standard of competence.

To do this, you must provide evidence to convince your assessor that you consistently meet **all** the performance criteria.

Your evidence must be the result of real work activities undertaken by yourself. Evidence from simulated activities is **not** acceptable for this element.

You must show evidence that you present your proposals in **both** the following **formats**
- written
- spoken.

Promote energy efficiency

Unit summary

This unit is about encouraging a culture of energy efficiency within the organisation and promoting the organisation's achievements in energy efficiency to outside audiences.

This unit contains two elements

E3.1 *Promote energy efficiency throughout the organisation*
E3.2 *Promote the organisation's achievements in energy efficiency.*

Personal competencies

In performing effectively in this unit, you will show that you

Acting strategically
- display an understanding of how the different parts of the organisation and its environment fit together
- clearly relate goals and actions to the strategic aims of the organisation
- take opportunities when they arise to achieve the longer-term aims or needs of your organisation

Communicating
- identify the information needs of listeners
- adopt communication styles appropriate to listeners and situations, including selecting an appropriate time and place
- use a variety of media and communication aids to reinforce points and maintain interest
- confirm listeners' understanding through questioning and interpretation of non-verbal signals
- modify communication in response to feedback from listeners

Influencing others
- present yourself positively to others
- create and prepare strategies for influencing others
- use a variety of means to influence others
- understand the culture of your organisation and act to work within it or influence it

Searching for information
- establish information networks to search for and gather relevant information
- make best use of existing sources of information
- seek information from multiple sources
- challenge the validity and reliability of sources of information.

Promote energy efficiency

Element E3.1

Promote energy efficiency throughout the organisation

Performance criteria

You must ensure that

a) you effectively communicate the **benefits** of energy efficiency to people throughout the organisation

b) you **promote** the organisation's achievements in energy efficiency throughout the organisation

c) you persuade **relevant people** to communicate their commitment to a culture of energy efficiency and energy conservation

d) there is a shared understanding of the role each part of the organisation must play in energy efficiency

e) you encourage individuals in the organisation to play an active role in the drive for energy efficiency.

Knowledge requirements

You need to know and understand

Communication
- the principles and processes of effective communication and how to apply them
- how to communicate the benefits of energy efficiency to relevant people in the organisation
- how to promote an understanding of, and enthusiasm for, energy efficiency

Energy efficiency
- the benefits of the efficient use of energy

Involvement and motivation
- how to gain people's commitment to energy efficiency

Organisational context
- the organisation's achievements in energy efficiency and how these came about
- people who could be influential in developing an energy efficient culture and how to gain their active support
- the structure of the organisation, the roles and responsibilities of teams and individuals within it.

Evidence requirements

You must prove that you *promote energy efficiency throughout the organisation* to the National Standard of competence.

To do this, you must provide evidence to convince your assessor that you consistently meet **all** the performance criteria.

Your evidence must be the result of real work activities undertaken by yourself. Evidence from simulated activities is **not** acceptable for this element.

You must show evidence that your advice is based on at least **two** of the following types of **benefits**
- costs
- quality
- productivity
- environment
- safety.

You must show evidence that you gain the commitment of at least **two** of the following types of **relevant people**
- colleagues working at the same level as yourself
- higher-level managers or sponsors
- technical specialists
- suppliers.

You must also show evidence that you **promote** energy efficiency using at least **two** of the following formats
- written
- graphic
- audio-visual
- electronic.

You must, however, convince your assessor that you have the necessary knowledge, understanding and skills to be able to perform competently in respect of **all** types of **benefits**, **relevant people** and **promotion** listed above.

Promote energy efficiency

Element E3.2

Promote the organisation's achievements in energy efficiency

Performance criteria

You must ensure that

a) you accurately evaluate opportunities to create and sustain awareness of energy efficiency outside the organisation

b) you seize opportunities which effectively **promote** awareness of energy efficiency, the organisation's achievements and policy

c) the information you provide on the organisation's achievements is up-to-date and consistent with the organisation's policy

d) the way you **promote** the organisation's energy policy and achievements emphasises how they contribute to its success

e) you encourage **appropriate people** to communicate their views and you reply to them effectively.

Knowledge requirements

You need to know and understand

Communication
- the range of opportunities available to create and sustain awareness of energy efficiency
- how to identify and evaluate opportunities to create and sustain awareness of energy efficiency outside the organisation
- how to emphasise the contribution which its energy policy and achievements make to the organisation's success
- the range of available presentational techniques and how to use them effectively
- how to encourage feedback and respond to it appropriately

Energy efficiency
- the principal techniques and technologies which support the efficient use of energy

Information handling
- how to check whether information is current

Organisational context
- the organisation's achievements in energy efficiency and how they came about
- the organisation's policies and procedures on the use of energy and on publicising its achievements.

Evidence requirements

You must prove that you *promote the organisation's achievements in energy efficiency* to the National Standard of competence.

To do this, you must provide evidence to convince your assessor that you consistently meet **all** the performance criteria.

Your evidence must be the result of real work activities undertaken by yourself. Evidence from simulated activities is **not** acceptable for this element.

You must show evidence that you **promote** the organisation's policy and achievements using at least **two** of the following formats
- written
- graphic
- audio-visual
- electronic.

You must also show evidence that you encourage feedback from at least **two** of the following types of **appropriate people**
- suppliers
- customers/service users
- special interest groups
- regulatory bodies
- the community.

You must, however, convince your assessor that you have the necessary knowledge, understanding and skills to be able to perform competently in respect of **all** types of **promotion** and **appropriate people** listed above.

Promote the importance and benefits of quality

Unit summary

This unit is about promoting the importance and benefits of quality throughout the organisation and its customer and supplier networks. It covers promoting the importance of quality to those who set the organisation's policies and strategies. It also covers publicising the benefits of quality and the organisation's quality achievements to audiences inside and outside the organisation.

This unit contains two elements

F1.1   *Promote the importance of quality in the organisation's strategy*

F1.2   *Promote quality throughout the organisation and its customer and supplier networks.*

Personal competencies

In performing effectively in this unit, you will show that you

Acting strategically
- display an understanding of how the different parts of the organisation and its environment fit together
- work towards a clearly defined vision of the future
- clearly relate goals and actions to the strategic aims of the organisation

Communicating
- adopt communication styles appropriate to listeners and situations, including selecting an appropriate time and place
- use a variety of media and communication aids to reinforce points and maintain interest
- present difficult ideas and problems in ways that promote understanding
- confirm listeners' understanding through questioning and interpretation of non-verbal signals
- encourage listeners to ask questions or rephrase statements to clarify their understanding
- modify communication in response to feedback from listeners

Influencing others
- present yourself positively to others
- create and prepare strategies for influencing others
- use a variety of means to influence others

Searching for information
- make best use of existing sources of information
- seek information from multiple sources
- challenge the validity and reliability of sources of information

Thinking and taking decisions
- identify a range of elements in and perspectives on a situation
- identify implications, consequences or causal relationships in a situation
- use your own experience and evidence from others to identify problems and understand situations.

Promote the importance and
benefits of quality

Element F1.1

Promote the importance of quality in the organisation's strategy

Performance criteria

You must ensure that

a) you accurately identify how quality can contribute to the organisation's vision, mission and values

b) you seize opportunities to link quality to the role and function of each part of the organisation

c) you present decision makers with **information** justifying the need for a focus on quality clearly, accurately, and with the appropriate degree of urgency

d) you enable decision makers to communicate their views about quality and you respond appropriately to these

e) your promotional methods present the case for quality clearly and publicise improvements the organisation has made

f) where your proposals for improvements are rejected, you identify the reasons and give suitable alternative options.

Knowledge requirements

You need to know and understand

Analytical techniques
- how to identify the reasons for proposals being rejected.

Communication
- the principles and processes of effective communication and how to apply them
- how to encourage and respond to feedback
- how to promote the case for quality
- how to publicise quality improvements made
- the importance of having alternative options available, in case original proposals are rejected.

Organisational context
- the organisation's vision, mission and values
- the organisation's structure and the responsibilities of people within it
- the key decision-makers and their preferred formats for the presentation of information.

Quality management
- how quality can contribute to an organisation's vision, mission and values
- the principal quality philosophies, concepts and methods
- the comparative advantages, disadvantages and applications of different quality concepts, standards, systems and programmes.

Strategic planning
- how organisational policies and strategies are developed, communicated and implemented.

Evidence requirements

You must prove that you *promote the importance of quality in the organisation's strategy* to the National Standard of competence.

To do this, you must provide evidence to convince your assessor that you consistently meet **all** the performance criteria.

Your evidence must be the result of real work activities undertaken by yourself. Evidence from simulated activities is acceptable **only** for performance criterion f) in this element.

You must show evidence that you present **two** of the following types of **information** justifying the need for a focus on quality
- opportunities for the organisation
- threats from competitors
- poor quality.

You must, however, convince your assessor that you have the necessary knowledge, understanding and skills to be able to perform competently in respect of **all** types of **information**, listed above.

Promote the importance and
benefits of quality

Element F1.2

Promote quality throughout the organisation and its customer and supplier networks

Performance criteria

You must ensure that

a) you accurately evaluate the extent to which increased awareness of quality may contribute to achieving the organisation's vision, mission and values

b) you consistently seize **opportunities** to promote awareness of quality, the organisation's quality achievements and its policies

c) the information you provide on the organisation's achievements and policies is up-to-date and consistent with its vision of quality

d) the way you **communicate** information emphasises how improvements in quality contribute to the organisation's success

e) you enable individuals in the organisation to understand their role in the drive for quality and help them make an active contribution

f) you use relevant and accurate information to reinforce the importance of quality in the continued improvement and effectiveness of the organisation

g) you encourage individuals to **communicate** their views on quality and you make appropriate responses to them.

Knowledge requirements

You need to know and understand

Analytical techniques
- how to evaluate the extent to which increased awareness of quality may contribute to the organisation's vision, mission and values.

Communication
- the principles and processes of effective communication and how to apply them
- how to identify and seize effective opportunities to promote awareness
- the range of available presentational techniques and how to use them effectively
- how to encourage feedback and respond to it appropriately.

Information handling
- how to check whether information is up-to-date.

Involvement and motivation
- how to encourage people to understand their role and make an active contribution to quality.

Organisational context
- the organisation's vision, mission and values
- the organisation's quality policies.

Quality management
- the range of opportunities available to create and sustain awareness of quality
- the organisation's quality achievements.

Evidence requirements

You must prove that you *promote quality throughout the organisation and its customer and supplier networks* to the National Standard of competence.

To do this, you must provide evidence to convince your assessor that you consistently meet **all** the performance criteria.

Your evidence must be the result of real work activities undertaken by yourself. Evidence from simulated activities is **not** acceptable for this element.

You must show evidence that you evaluate at least **two** of the following types of **opportunities**
- training and development
- publicity
- customer and supplier awareness campaigns
- product or service improvement programmes.

You must also show evidence that you **communicate** to at least **two** of the following groups
- employees
- internal customers
- external customers
- suppliers.

You must, however, convince your assessor that you have the necessary knowledge, understanding and skills to be able to perform competently in respect of **all** types of **opportunities** and groups you **communicate** with, listed above.

Manage continuous quality improvement

Unit summary

This unit is about ensuring there is continuous quality improvement throughout the organisation. It covers the development of systems to evaluate organisational performance and promoting continuous quality improvements in the organisation's products, services and processes.

This unit contains two elements

F3.1 *Develop and implement systems to monitor and evaluate organisational performance*

F3.2 *Promote continuous quality improvement for products, services and processes.*

Personal competencies

In performing effectively in this unit, you will show that you

Acting strategically
- clearly relate goals and actions to the strategic aims of the organisation
- take opportunities when they arise to achieve the longer-term aims or needs of the organisation

Communicating
- listen actively, ask questions, clarify points and rephrase others' statements to check mutual understanding
- identify the information needs of listeners
- adopt communication styles appropriate to listeners and situations, including selecting an appropriate time and place

Focusing on results
- use change as an opportunity for improvement
- establish and communicate high expectations of performance, including setting an example to others
- set goals that are demanding of self and others
- monitor quality of work and progress against plans
- continually strive to identify and minimise barriers to excellence

Influencing others
- create and prepare strategies for influencing others
- use a variety of means to influence others
- understand the culture of the organisation and act to work within it or influence it

Searching for information
- seek information from multiple sources
- challenge the validity and reliability of sources of information

Thinking and taking decisions
- break processes down into tasks and activities
- use your own experience and evidence from others to identify problems and understand situations
- identify patterns or meaning from events and data which are not obviously related
- build a total and valid picture from restricted or incomplete data
- take decisions which are realistic for the situation.

Manage continuous quality improvement

Develop and implement systems to monitor and evaluate organisational performance

Performance criteria

You must ensure that

a) you agree the scope and objectives of the system to monitor and evaluate organisational performance with **relevant people**

b) you develop a system which takes account of all critical factors

c) you identify appropriate performance measures and assessment tools and techniques

d) you identify and confirm existing and potential sources of **information**

e) you obtain and provide sufficient resources for the system to be effective

f) where it is not possible to obtain or provide sufficient resources, the objectives and scope are modified with the agreement of **relevant people**

g) monitoring and evaluation systems are clearly, accurately and comprehensively documented

h) you give **relevant people** adequate and accurate **information** about the evaluation

i) where you use a sampling approach, it is justifiable in terms of technique, cost and the data likely to be obtained.

Knowledge requirements

You need to know and understand

Analytical techniques

- the range of appropriate assessment tools and techniques, their relative advantages and disadvantages and how to decide which to use
- the range of appropriate sampling techniques, their relative advantages and disadvantages and how to decide which to use
- how to justify the use of sampling techniques in terms of cost and the data likely to be obtained.

Information handling

- existing and potential sources of information and how to access them
- the importance of clear, accurate and comprehensive documentation and how to achieve this.

Monitoring and evaluation

- performance measures and how to develop them.

Organisational context

- relevant people to involve in the development and implementation of monitoring and evaluation systems
- the critical factors which need to be taken into account when developing the system and how to identify them.

Resource management

- how to identify the resources needed for the system and how to obtain these resources.

Evidence requirements

You must prove that you *develop and implement systems to monitor and evaluate organisational performance* to the National Standard of competence.

To do this, you must provide evidence to convince your assessor that you consistently meet **all** the performance criteria.

Your evidence must be the result of real work activities undertaken by yourself. Evidence from simulated activities is acceptable **only** for performance criteria f) and i) in this element.

You must show evidence that you involve at least **two** of the following types of **relevant people**

- higher level managers or sponsors
- colleagues working at the same level as yourself
- quality specialists.

You must also show evidence that you identify sources of **information** about **all** of the following

- products
- services
- processes
- customers
- suppliers.

You must, however, convince your assessor that you have the necessary knowledge, understanding and skills to be able to perform competently in respect of **all** types of **relevant people**, listed above.

Manage continuous quality improvement

Element F3.2

Promote continuous quality improvement for products, services and processes

Performance criteria

You must ensure that

a) you assess the outcomes of continuous monitoring and quality evaluations for their implications for the organisation

b) you correctly identify **trends and developments** in the quality of products, services and processes

c) you advise **relevant people** promptly about the impact **trends and developments** may have on the perceived and actual quality of the organisation's products, services and processes

d) you make recommendations for improving the quality of products, services and processes to **relevant people** in a form which supports decision-making

e) your recommendations clearly show the benefits which **improvements** could bring against the resources which would need to be expended

f) you obtain and provide sufficient resources and support to allow **improvements** to be implemented successfully

g) you monitor **improvements** for their effectiveness against agreed criteria

h) you encourage **relevant people** to be involved in continuous quality improvement.

Knowledge requirements

You need to know and understand

Analytical techniques
- how to conduct a cost-benefit analysis.

Communication
- the principles and processes of effective communication and how to apply them
- how to make recommendations in a form which supports decision-making.

Involvement and motivation
- how to motivate individuals to be involved in continuous quality improvement.

Monitoring and evaluation
- the relevant information from performance monitoring and evaluation systems
- how to assess the implications of the results of monitoring and evaluation for the organisation
- the relevant trends and developments, both inside and outside the organisation
- how to develop criteria to measure effectiveness.

Organisational context
- the people who should be involved in decisions on continuous quality improvement and how to secure their involvement.

Quality management
- how to assess the impact of trends and developments on the perceived or actual quality of the organisation's products, services and processes.

Resource management
- how to assess the resources needed to implement improvements, and how to obtain and provide these resources.

Evidence requirements

You must prove that you *promote continuous quality improvement for products, services and processes* to the National Standard of competence.

To do this, you must provide evidence to convince your assessor that you consistently meet **all** the performance criteria.

Your evidence must be the result of real work activities undertaken by yourself. Evidence from simulated activities is **not** acceptable for this element.

You must show evidence that you identify **both** of the following types of **trends and developments**
- internal
- external.

You must show evidence that you involve at least **two** of the following types of **relevant people**
- higher-level managers or sponsors
- colleagues working at the same level as yourself
- quality specialists.

You must also show evidence that you recommend and implement **all** of the following types of **improvements**
- improvements in human performance
- improvements in systems performance
- improvements in organisational policies and strategies.

You must, however, convince your assessor that you have the necessary knowledge, understanding and skills to be able to perform competently in respect of **all** types of **relevant people**, listed above.

Implement quality assurance systems

Unit summary

This unit is about ensuring that your organisation's products and services continuously meet the standard required by your customers. It covers setting up quality assurance systems, assuring quality by making sure these systems operate effectively and making recommendations for improvements to quality assurance systems.

This unit contains three elements

F4.1 *Establish quality assurance systems*
F4.2 *Maintain quality assurance systems*
F4.3 *Recommend improvements to quality assurance systems.*

Personal competencies

In performing effectively in this unit, you will show that you

Communicating
- listen actively, ask questions, clarify points and rephrase others' statements to check mutual understanding
- adopt communication styles appropriate to listeners and situations, including selecting an appropriate time and place
- encourage listeners to ask questions or rephrase statements to clarify their understanding

Focusing on results
- actively seek to do things better
- use change as an opportunity for improvement
- establish and communicate high expectations of performance, including setting an example to others
- monitor quality of work and progress against plans

Influencing others
- present yourself positively to others
- create and prepare strategies for influencing others
- use a variety of means to influence others
- understand the culture of the organisation and act to work within it or influence it

Thinking and taking decisions
- break processes down into tasks and activities
- use your own experience and evidence from others to identify problems and understand situations
- identify patterns or meaning from events and data which are not obviously related
- produce a variety of solutions before taking a decision
- produce your own ideas from experience and practice
- take decisions which are realistic for the situation.

**Implement quality assurance
systems**

Element F4.1

Establish quality
assurance systems

Performance criteria

You must ensure that

a) your analysis of processes is sufficient to determine appropriate **quality assurance systems** and measurements

b) you present your recommendations and rationale for establishing **quality assurance systems** to **relevant people** with the appropriate level of detail and degree of urgency

c) you agree implementation plans, taking account of feedback from **relevant people**

d) you provide opportunities for those involved in **quality assurance systems** to contribute to their development

e) the systems you set up clearly specify the processes, procedures and measurements required to ensure products and services are within the limits of acceptable quality

f) your **quality assurance systems** are capable of making sure that agreed customer requirements are consistently met

g) you **communicate** the establishment of **quality assurance systems** in a way which is clear, detailed and allows adequate time for preparation

h) you **communicate** the results and benefits of assuring quality at times most likely to gain the commitment of **relevant people** to the systems.

Knowledge requirements

You need to know and understand

Communication
- how to communicate effectively to colleagues, team members and higher-level managers and sponsors on quality assurance issues.

Customer relations
- the importance of customer focus in managing quality.

Involvement and motivation
- how to develop and present an effective case for the introduction of quality assurance systems
- the importance of consulting on the introduction of quality assurance systems and how to do so effectively
- how to gain the commitment of staff for quality assurance systems.

Quality management
- the importance of quality assurance and your role and responsibility in relation to this
- the meaning of quality in the context of managing activities
- the principles underpinning effective quality assurance systems and how to apply them
- the range of quality assurance systems available and their relative advantages and disadvantages to the activities for which you are responsible
- how to analyse work processes and determine the most appropriate quality assurance systems and measurements
- how to specify the requirements of a quality assurance system.

Evidence requirements

You must prove that you *establish quality assurance systems* to the National Standard of competence.

To do this, you must provide evidence to convince your assessor that you consistently meet **all** the performance criteria.

Your evidence must be the result of real work activities undertaken by yourself. Evidence from simulated activities is **not** acceptable for this element.

You must show evidence that you have established at least **one** of the following types of **quality assurance systems**
- externally validated
- devised and validated in-house.

You must show evidence of your work in this area with at least **three** of the following types of **relevant people**
- team members
- colleagues working at the same level as you
- higher-level managers or sponsors
- specialists.

You must also show evidence that your **communications** are in at least **two** of the following forms
- spoken
- written
- images.

You must, however, convince your assessor that you have the necessary knowledge, understanding and skills to be able to perform competently in respect of **all** types of **quality assurance systems, relevant people** and **communications**, listed above.

Implement quality assurance
systems

Element F4.2

Maintain quality assurance systems

Performance criteria

You must ensure that

a) you present information on **quality assurance systems**, procedures and responsibilities to **relevant people** at a time and place and in a format appropriate to their needs

b) you confirm **relevant people's** understanding of, and commitment to, **quality assurance systems** at appropriate intervals

c) you collect and **evaluate** information, and report the results at required intervals, using agreed methods and against specified performance measures

d) you take prompt and effective action to clarify inadequate, contradictory or ambiguous information

e) you actively encourage **relevant people** freely to report actual and potential variations in quality

f) you take timely and effective action, consistent with quality assurance procedures, to rectify unacceptable variations in products and services.

Knowledge requirements

You need to know and understand

Communication

- how to communicate effectively with team members, colleagues and higher-level managers and sponsors on quality assurance issues.

Information handling

- how to validate information which may be inadequate, contradictory and ambiguous.

Involvement and motivation

- how to maintain staff commitment to quality assurance systems
- how to encourage and enable feedback on quality.

Quality management

- the importance of maintaining quality assurance systems and the procedures required to do so.

Evidence requirements

You must prove that you *maintain quality assurance systems* to the National Standard of competence.

To do this, you must provide evidence to convince your assessor that you consistently meet **all** the performance criteria.

Your evidence must be the result of real work activities undertaken by yourself. Evidence from simulated activities is acceptable **only** for performance criteria d) and f) in this element.

You must show evidence that you maintain **one** of the following types of **quality assurance systems**

- externally validated
- devised and validated in-house.

You must also show evidence of your work in this area with at least *three* of the following types of **relevant people**

- team members
- colleagues working at the same level as you
- higher-level managers or sponsors
- specialists.

You must also show evidence that you use **both** the following types of **evaluation** methods

- qualitative
- quantitative.

You must, however, convince your assessor that you have the necessary knowledge, understanding and skills to be able to perform competently in respect of **all** types of **quality assurance systems**, and **relevant people**, listed above.

Implement quality assurance
systems

Element F4.3

Recommend improvements to quality assurance systems

Performance criteria

You must ensure that

a) you provide opportunities for **relevant people** to suggest improvements to **quality assurance systems**

b) you base your **recommendations** on sufficient, valid and reliable information on the effectiveness and efficiency of **quality assurance systems**

c) your **recommendations** have the potential to improve the contribution which **quality assurance systems** make to the organisation and its customers

d) you present your **recommendations** to **relevant people** clearly, logically and in time to be of use

e) where **recommendations** are not accepted, you establish the reasons and present these to **relevant people** in a manner which maintains morale and motivation.

Knowledge requirements

You need to know and understand

Communication

- how to communicate effectively with team members, colleagues and higher-level managers and sponsors on quality assurance issues
- how to develop and argue an effective case for change.

Continuous improvement

- the importance of continuous improvement to the effectiveness of the team and organisation and your role and responsibilities in relation to this.

Customer relations

- the importance of customer focus in managing activities.

Involvement and motivation

- how to encourage and enable feedback on quality systems.

Information handling

- how to collect and validate sufficient information on the effectiveness of quality assurance systems to make recommendations on improvement.

Working relationships

- how to resolve disagreements and disputes in ways which maintain morale and motivation.

Evidence requirements

You must prove that you *recommend improvements to quality assurance systems* to the National Standard of competence.

To do this, you must provide evidence to convince your assessor that you consistently meet **all** the performance criteria.

Your evidence must be the result of real work activities undertaken by yourself. Evidence from simulated activities is acceptable **only** for performance criterion e) in this element.

You must show evidence that you have recommended improvements for at least **one** of the following types of **quality assurance systems**

- externally validated
- devised and validated in-house.

You must also show evidence that you work with at least **three** of the following types of **relevant people**

- team members
- colleagues working at the same level as you
- higher-level managers or sponsors
- specialists.

You must also show evidence that you make **both** of the following types of **recommendations**

- in response to request
- on own initiative.

You must, however, convince your assessor that you have the necessary knowledge, understanding and skills to be able to perform competently in respect of **all** types of **quality assurance systems**, and **relevant people**, listed above.

Monitor compliance with quality systems

Unit summary

This unit is about ensuring that all the processes of the organisation comply with quality systems. It covers planning to audit quality systems, implementing this plan and providing a report on the organisation's overall compliance with its quality systems.

This unit contains three elements

F6.1 *Plan to audit compliance with quality systems*
F6.2 *Implement the audit plan*
F6.3 *Report on compliance with quality systems.*

Personal competencies

In performing effectively in this unit, you will show that you

Building teams
- make time available to support others
- encourage and stimulate others to make the best use of their abilities
- evaluate and enhance people's capability to do their jobs
- provide feedback designed to improve people's future performance
- show respect for the views and actions of others
- show sensitivity to the needs and feelings of others
- use power and authority in a fair and equitable manner

Communicating
- listen actively, ask questions, clarify points and rephrase others' statements to check mutual understanding
- identify the information needs of listeners
- adopt communication styles appropriate to listeners and situations, including selecting an appropriate time and place

Focusing on results
- maintain a focus on objectives
- tackle problems and take advantage of opportunities as they arise
- prioritise objectives and schedule work to make best use of time and resources

Searching for information
- seek information from multiple sources
- challenge the validity and reliability of sources of information

Thinking and taking decisions
- break processes down into tasks and activities
- use your own experience and evidence from others to identify problems and understand situations
- identify patterns or meaning from events and data which are not obviously related
- build a total and valid picture from restricted or incomplete data
- take decisions which are realistic for the situation.

Monitor compliance with quality systems

Element F6.1

Plan to audit compliance with quality systems

Performance criteria

You must ensure that

a) you agree the scope and objectives of the **audits** with **relevant people**

b) you accurately identify processes in the organisation where non-compliance is most likely

c) you accurately identify the relative risks to the organisation of non-compliance with quality systems in each of the organisation's processes

d) you agree with **relevant people** a programme of **audits** which prioritises areas of greatest risk and likely non-compliance

e) you develop a sufficient number of competent people to carry out the programme of **audits**

f) your programme of **audits** complies with the organisation's quality policies and procedures.

Knowledge requirements

You need to know and understand

Analytical techniques
- how to assess the relative risks of non-compliance with quality systems.

Communication
- the principles and processes of effective communication and how to apply them.

Organisational context
- the relevant structures, responsibilities and processes within the organisation
- the people within the organisation with whom you must agree the scope, objectives and programme of audits
- the organisation's quality policy and procedures.

Quality management
- the principles of quality auditing and how to conduct an audit investigation
- how to agree the scope and objectives of quality audits
- how to assess which of the organisation's processes are likely not to comply with quality systems
- the knowledge and skills required by those who will carry out the audits, and how to assess and develop these skills and knowledge.

Evidence requirements

You must prove that you *plan to audit compliance with quality systems* to the National Standard of competence.

To do this, you must provide evidence to convince your assessor that you consistently meet **all** the performance criteria.

Your evidence must be the result of real work activities undertaken by yourself. Evidence from simulated activities is **not** acceptable for this element.

You must show evidence that you plan **one** of the following types of **audits**
- within your organisation
- in other organisations.

You must also show evidence that you agree the scope, objectives and programme of the audits with **one** of the following types of **relevant people**
- higher-level managers or sponsors
- colleagues working at the same level as yourself
- quality specialists.

You must, however, convince your assessor that you have the necessary knowledge, understanding and skills to be able to perform competently in respect of **all** types of **audits** and **relevant people**, listed above.

Monitor compliance with quality systems

Element F6.2

Implement the audit plan

Performance criteria

You must ensure that

a) you allocate **audits** to competent people, taking account of their expertise, development needs and the need to provide equal opportunities

b) you provide sufficient support and advice to auditors to allow them to work effectively yet autonomously

c) you regularly monitor the progress of **audit** activity against the plan, and take appropriate **corrective action** in the event of significant variations

d) you provide **relevant people** with regular reports of progress against the plan.

Knowledge requirements

You need to know and understand

Communication
- the principles and processes of effective communication and how to apply them
- how to present progress reports

Equal opportunities
- the principles, organisational policies, values and legal requirements affecting equal opportunities at work.

Monitoring and evaluation
- how to monitor activities against plans, identify significant variations and decide on appropriate corrective action.

Organisational context
- the relevant structures, responsibilities and processes within the organisation
- the organisation's quality policy and procedures.

Quality management
- the principles of quality auditing and how to conduct an audit investigation
- the knowledge and skills required by those who will carry out the audits, and how to assess and develop these skills and knowledge.

Team working
- how to allocate work to a team based on their expertise, development needs and the need to provide equal opportunities for development to all competent people
- how to identify and provide the support and advice people need in order to work effectively yet autonomously.

Evidence requirements

You must prove that you *implement the audit plan* to the National Standard of competence.

To do this, you must provide evidence to convince your assessor that you consistently meet **all** the performance criteria.

Your evidence must be the result of real work activities undertaken by yourself. Evidence from simulated activities is acceptable **only** for performance criterion c) in this element.

You must show evidence that you implement **one** of the following types of **audits**
- within your organisation
- in other organisations.

You must also show evidence that you take **one** of the following types of **corrective action**
- changing audit activities
- changing the way resources are used for audit activities
- renegotiating the programme of audits.

You must also show evidence that you provide regular progress reports to **one** of the following types of **relevant people**
- higher-level managers or sponsors
- colleagues working at the same level as yourself
- quality specialists.

You must, however, convince your assessor that you have the necessary knowledge, understanding and skills to be able to perform competently in respect of **all** types of **audits**, **corrective action** and **relevant people**, listed above.

Monitor compliance with quality systems

Element F6.3

Report on compliance with quality systems

Performance criteria

You must ensure that

a) you accurately evaluate the results of quality **audits** against the organisation's quality objectives, relevant standards, legal requirements and industry best practice

b) you fully assess the appropriateness of the corrective action agreed to deal with discrepancies found during **audits**

c) you advise **relevant people**, with the appropriate level of urgency, of the risks associated with non-compliance discovered during **audits**

d) you report the findings of your evaluation to **relevant people** in accordance with organisational requirements

e) you give feedback to those whose performance was audited in a way which enhances their confidence and commitment to quality

f) you accurately assess your auditors' performance and implement appropriate development activities.

Knowledge requirements

You need to know and understand

Communication

- the principles and processes of effective communication and how to apply them
- how to report your findings
- how to give feedback in a way which enhances confidence and commitment.

Monitoring and evaluation

- how to evaluate the results of quality audits against the organisation's quality objectives, relevant standards, statutory requirements and industry best practice
- how to assess the appropriateness of corrective actions agreed.

Organisational context

- the relevant structures, responsibilities and processes within the organisation
- the organisation's quality objectives, policy and procedures
- the organisation's requirements for reporting on compliance with quality systems.

Quality management

- the principles of quality auditing and how to conduct an audit investigation
- how to assess the performance of auditors
- the knowledge and skills required by those who will carry out the audits, and how to assess and develop these skills and knowledge.

Evidence requirements

You must prove that you *report on compliance with quality systems* to the National Standard of competence.

To do this, you must provide evidence to convince your assessor that you consistently meet **all** the performance criteria.

Your evidence must be the result of real work activities undertaken by yourself. Evidence from simulated activities is **not** acceptable for this element.

You must show evidence that you evaluate the results of **one** of the following types of **audits**
- within your organisation
- in other organisations.

You must also show evidence that you report the findings of your evaluation to **one** of the following types of **relevant people**
- higher-level managers or sponsors
- colleagues working at the same level as yourself
- quality specialists.

You must, however, convince your assessor that you have the necessary knowledge, understanding and skills to be able to perform competently in respect of **all** types of **audits** and **relevant people**, listed above.

Plan and prepare projects

Unit summary

This unit is about planning and setting up substantial, complex projects which are critical to the strategic objectives of the sponsoring organisation. Project sponsors may be internal or external to your organisation.

This unit contains three elements

G4.1 *Agree the project's scope and definition with the sponsor*
G4.2 *Develop plans to achieve the project's goals*
G4.3 *Establish the project's resourcing and control methods.*

Personal competencies

In performing effectively in this unit, you will show that you

Acting strategically

- display an understanding of how the different parts of the organisation and its environment fit together
- work towards a clearly defined vision of the future
- clearly relate your goals and actions to the strategic aims of the organisation
- take opportunities when they arise to achieve the longer-term aims or needs of the organisation

Communicating

- listen actively, ask questions, clarify points and rephrase others' statements to check mutual understanding

Focusing on results

- maintain a focus on objectives
- tackle problems and take advantage of opportunities as they arise
- prioritise objectives and schedule work to make the best use of time and resources

Influencing others

- develop and use contacts to trade information, and obtain support and resources
- present yourself positively to others
- create and prepare strategies for influencing others
- use a variety of means to influence others

Thinking and taking decisions

- produce a variety of solutions before taking a decision
- reconcile and make use of a variety of perspectives when making sense of a situation
- produce your own ideas from experience and practice
- take decisions which are realistic for the situation.

Plan and prepare projects

Element G4.1

Agree the project's scope and definition with the sponsor

Performance criteria

You must ensure that

a) you clarify the **project's** scope and definition to the level of detail needed to plan the **project** effectively

b) you identify the main links between the **project's** scope and definition and the sponsor's strategic and operational objectives

c) you identify and reconcile key **stakeholders'** interests in the **project**

d) you identify the main contingencies which may occur during the running of the **project** and assess their likely impact

e) you identify, assess and prioritise the main risks associated with the **project**

f) you assess the **project's** feasibility and negotiate any necessary amendments with the sponsor in a way which ensures the goals can be achieved within **constraints**

g) you clearly establish your own level of authority and accountability for **project** activities, resources and decisions

h) you clearly confirm all aspects of the **project's** scope and definition with the sponsor.

Knowledge requirements

You need to know and understand

Analytical techniques

- risk identification and assessment in project planning and how to prioritise risks

Customer relations

- the importance of clarifying and agreeing the project's scope and definition and how to do this with a sponsor
- the importance of maintaining effective working relationships with sponsors and how to do so
- the importance of establishing your own level of authority in the project
- how to re-negotiate project definitions with sponsors

Organisational context

- how projects interlink with and support organisations' wider strategic and operational objectives and the importance of being aware of such links

Planning

- the importance of systematic and thorough planning to the success of projects
- the level of detail needed to start systematic project planning
- the types of constraints which usually exist in projects (for example, time, resources, technology and legislation) and how to look for and assess the significance of constraints
- the importance of making an initial assessment of the feasibility of projects and how to do so
- the importance of planning for contingencies and how to do so.

Evidence requirements

You must prove that you *agree the project's scope and definition with the sponsor* to the National Standard of competence.

To do this, you must provide evidence to convince your assessor that you consistently meet **all** the performance criteria.

Your evidence must be the result of real work activities undertaken by yourself. Evidence from simulated activities is **only** acceptable for performance criterion f).

You must show evidence that you agree the scope and definition for at least **two** of the following types of **projects**

- with strategic implications for the sponsor
- with substantial resource implications for the sponsor
- with a high level of complexity
- involving external organisations.

You must also show evidence that you identify and negotiate within **three** of the following types of **constraints**

- time
- resources
- available techniques
- organisational policies
- statutory and regulatory requirements.

You must also show evidence that you identify **both** of the following types of **stakeholders** and their interests

- internal
- external.

You must, however, convince your assessor that you have the necessary knowledge, understanding and skills to be able to perform competently in respect of **all** types of **projects** and **constraints** listed above.

Plan and prepare projects

Element G4.2

Develop plans to achieve the project's goals

Performance criteria

You must ensure that

a) you involve **relevant people** in the development of the **project** plans and accurately record all aspects of the planning process

b) the strategy and plans for the **project** are consistent with the agreed scope, definition and known **constraints**

c) the plans break the **project** work down into tasks which are manageable, measurable, and achievable

d) the plans correctly identify links, dependencies, schedules, evaluation methods, deliverables and handover procedures

e) the plans include effective measures to deal with identified contingencies and risks

f) the plans realistically estimate and cost the human and physical resources required to carry out the **project's** tasks

g) you base the plans on previous experience and the good practice of others

h) you check, negotiate and agree all key aspects of the **project** plans with the sponsor and obtain authorisation to proceed.

Knowledge requirements

You need to know and understand

Planning

- the principles underpinning effective project planning
- different models of project planning and management
- the people to involve in developing project plans
- how to break the work down into manageable, achievable and measurable tasks
- how to estimate and cost the human and physical resources needed for projects
- the importance of identifying schedule, links, dependencies, monitoring and evaluation methods and handover and how to do so
- the importance of contingency and risk planning and how to do so
- how computer-based project planning approaches may be used
- the importance of using your own past experience and that of others and how to research and identify good practice

Working relationships

- the skills required to negotiate with relevant people involved in the project
- the importance of agreeing and recording the project's plans with relevant people
- the importance of obtaining authorisation before proceeding.

Evidence requirements

You must prove that you *develop plans to achieve the project's goals* to the National Standard of competence.

To do this, you must provide evidence to convince your assessor that you consistently meet **all** the performance criteria.

Your evidence must be the result of real work activities undertaken by yourself. Evidence from simulated activities is **not** acceptable for this element.

You must show evidence that you involve at least **two** of the following types of **relevant people**
- team members
- colleagues
- specialists.

You must show evidence that you develop plans for at least **two** of the following types of **projects**
- with strategic implications for the sponsor
- with substantial resource implications for the sponsor
- with a high level of complexity
- involving external organisations.

You must also show evidence that your plans take account of at least **two** of the following types of **constraints**
- time
- resources
- available techniques
- organisational policies
- statutory and regulatory requirements.

You must, however, convince your assessor that you have the necessary knowledge, understanding and skills to be able to perform competently in respect of **all** types of **relevant people**, **projects** and **constraints** listed above.

Plan and prepare projects

Establish the project's resourcing and control methods

Performance criteria

You must ensure that

a) your selected **team members** are able to make an effective contribution to the **project's** objectives

b) the roles assigned to **team members**, and the tasks they are allocated, are realistic and equitable

c) the **team members'** lines of responsibility and accountability are clear, unambiguous and take account of their other responsibilities

d) there are agreed meeting schedules, reporting, control and communication methods which are consistent with the **project** plans

e) there are effective opportunities for team development

f) the methods of obtaining and managing the necessary **resources** are efficient, effective and consistent with legal and organisational requirements.

Knowledge requirements

You need to know and understand

Communications
- the importance of having good communications and how to maximise the effectiveness and efficiency of communications

Delegation
- how to allocate project roles and tasks equitably and realistically
- the importance of having clear lines of responsibility and accountability within the project and how to establish these, especially where line management responsibility is shared
- the importance and purpose of control methods and how to select methods appropriate to different types of projects

Organisational context
- the organisational and legal requirements which are relevant to managing resources and finance

Recruitment and selection
- how to identify and specify the competences, skills and knowledge which project team members need
- how to obtain the people you require to staff projects

Resource management
- the importance of tight financial and resource controls, and the methods which may be used

Training and development
- the importance of team development and methods to achieve this.

Evidence requirements

You must prove that you *establish the project's resourcing and control methods* to the National Standard of competence.

To do this, you must provide evidence to convince your assessor that you consistently meet **all** the performance criteria.

Your evidence must be the result of real work activities undertaken by yourself. Evidence from simulated activities is **not** acceptable for this element.

You must show evidence that you involve at least **two** of the following types of **team members**
- people exclusively involved in the project
- people who have other responsibilities and accountabilities
- people from outside your organisation.

You must also show evidence that you establish resourcing and control for at least **two** of the following types of **projects**
- with strategic implications for the sponsor
- with substantial resource implications for the sponsor
- with a high level of complexity
- involving external organisations.

You must show evidence that you have methods to obtain and manage **both** of the following types of **resources**
- from within your organisation
- from outside your organisation.

You must, however, convince your assessor that you have the necessary knowledge, understanding and skills to be able to perform competently in respect of **all** types of **team members** and **projects** listed above.

Manage the running of projects

Unit summary

This unit is about managing the work of substantial, complex projects which are critical to the strategic objectives of the sponsoring organisation. Project sponsors may be internal or external to your organisation.

This unit contains four elements

G5.1 *Lead the project team*
G5.2 *Monitor and adjust activities, resources and plans*
G5.3 *Develop solutions to project problems*
G5.4 *Maintain communication with project stakeholders.*

Personal competencies

In performing effectively in this unit, you will show that you

Acting assertively
- take a leading role in initiating action and making decisions
- take personal responsibility for making things happen
- take control of situations and events
- act in an assured and unhesitating manner when faced with a challenge
- state your own position and views clearly in conflict situations

Communicating
- listen actively, ask questions, clarify points and rephrase others' statements to check mutual understanding
- identify the information needs of listeners
- adopt communication styles appropriate to listeners and situations, including selecting an appropriate time and place
- use a variety of media and communication aids to reinforce points and maintain interest
- present difficult ideas and problems in ways that promote understanding

Focusing on results
- maintain a focus on objectives
- tackle problems and take advantage of opportunities as they arise
- prioritise objectives and schedule work to make the best use of time and resources

Thinking and taking decisions
- produce a variety of solutions before taking a decision
- reconcile and make use of a variety of perspectives when making sense of a situation
- produce your own ideas from experience and practice
- take decisions which are realistic for the situation.

Manage the running of projects

Element G5.1

Lead the project team

Performance criteria

You must ensure that

a) you consistently motivate **team members** to fulfil the tasks allocated to them with commitment and enthusiasm

b) your **team members** consistently receive clear, accurate and up-to-date information appropriate to the role which they will play in the **project**

c) you delegate responsibilities to others in ways which make best use of the team's resources

d) your **team members** and **stakeholders** have effective opportunities to contribute to the development of the **project**

e) you correctly and promptly identify problems which **team members** and **stakeholders** are experiencing

f) your **team members** receive the support they need to achieve their objectives throughout the lifetime of the **project**.

Knowledge requirements

You need to know and understand

Involvement and motivation
- methods which may be used to motivate team members and gain their commitment
- how to delegate project responsibilities effectively on a day-to-day basis
- the importance of keeping team members properly informed as to their roles in the project and effective methods to make this happen
- the importance of enabling team members to contribute to the development of the project and different methods of achieving this

Leadership styles
- the principles which underpin the effective leadership of projects and your role in relation to this
- styles of leadership which are effective in managing projects

Providing support
- the importance of providing support to team members during projects
- the types of problems which team members and stakeholders may experience
- the types of support which team members may need during projects and how to identify and provide such support.

Evidence requirements

You must prove that you *lead the project team* to the National Standard of competence.

To do this, you must provide evidence to convince your assessor that you consistently meet **all** the performance criteria.

Your evidence must be the result of real work activities undertaken by yourself. Evidence from simulated activities is **not** acceptable for this element.

You must show evidence that you lead at least **two** of the following types of **projects**
- with strategic implications for the sponsor
- with substantial resource implications for the sponsor
- with a high level of complexity
- involving external organisations.

You must show evidence that you work with at least **two** of the following types of **team members**
- people exclusively involved in the project
- people who have other responsibilities and accountabilities
- people from outside your organisation.

You must also show evidence that you work with **both** of the following types of **stakeholders**
- internal
- external.

You must, however, convince your assessor that you have the necessary knowledge, understanding and skills to be able to perform competently in respect of **all** types of **projects** and **team members** listed above.

Manage the running of projects

Element G5.2

Monitor and adjust activities, resources and plans

Performance criteria

You must ensure that

a) you **monitor** and **evaluate** project work in a way which is consistent with your plans, and enables the **project** to achieve its goals

b) your **evaluation** accurately measures progress against plans and identifies emerging risks, difficulties and their causes

c) you provide clear authorisation for all stages of work to begin, continue and finish on the basis of your plans and your **evaluation** of progress

d) you keep the **project** activities and resources in line with your plans or adjust your plans in a way which is consistent with the **project's** scope and definition

e) you actively seek and **evaluate** ways to improve the work of the **project**, and control changes in a way which keeps disruption to a minimum

f) any adjustments to activities, resources and plans are made with the knowledge and agreement of **team members** and sponsors and are accurately recorded and securely stored

g) you inform the **project** sponsor promptly and clearly of any need to review the **project** scope and definition.

Knowledge requirements

You need to know and understand

Analytical techniques
- how to identify and assess emerging risks

Change management
- how to identify and evaluate ways of improving project work
- the importance of managing change in projects and how to minimise disruption wherever possible

Project management
- different project management methods and how to select methods appropriate to your own circumstances
- methods to monitor and evaluate project progress effectively
- the importance of authorising all stages of work to start, continue or finish according to your evaluation of progress
- the importance of keeping activities in line with the plans for the project and methods to control this

Resource management
- why resources need to be tightly controlled and methods to achieve this

Working relationships
- the importance of keeping project sponsors informed of any implications for the project's scope and definition
- the importance of obtaining team members' agreement to changes in plans
- the people who need to be consulted on changes
- how to negotiate adjustments to the satisfaction of all those involved.

Evidence requirements

You must prove that you *monitor and adjust activities, resources and plans* to the National Standard of competence.

To do this, you must provide evidence to convince your assessor that you consistently meet **all** the performance criteria.

Your evidence must be the result of real work activities undertaken by yourself. Evidence from simulated activities is **only** acceptable for performance criterion g).

You must show evidence that you use **both** of the following types of **monitoring** and **evaluation**
- by direct observation of activities
- by considering reports from others.

You must also show evidence that you monitor and control at least **two** of the following types of **projects**
- with strategic implications for the sponsor
- with substantial resource implications for the sponsor
- with a high level of complexity
- involving external organisations.

You must show evidence that you work with at least **two** of the following types of **team members**
- people exclusively involved in the project
- people who have other responsibilities and accountabilities
- people from outside your organisation.

You must, however, convince your assessor that you have the necessary knowledge, understanding and skills to be able to perform competently in respect of **all** types of **team members** and **projects** listed above.

Manage the running of projects

Element G5.3

Develop solutions to project problems

Performance criteria

You must ensure that

a) you collate and verify all information necessary and relevant to the **problem** in a way which facilitates effective and efficient analysis

b) you analyse the available information from the perspectives of all major stakeholders, identifying and prioritising all known factors according to the **project** scope and definition

c) you provide **team members** and sponsors with opportunities to contribute effectively to the development of solutions

d) you develop and present a range of solutions compatible with the **project** scope and definition, drawing on your own experience and the good practice of others

e) your proposed solutions make efficient and effective use of the resources available

f) you clearly present the range of solutions to **team members** and sponsors, objectively outlining the strengths and weaknesses of each, according to the **project** scope and definition

g) you select an optimum solution and obtain the support of **team members** and sponsors.

Knowledge requirements

You need to know and understand

Analytical techniques
- the principles underpinning effective problem-solving
- the importance of collecting as much relevant information as possible and collating such information in a way which facilitates decision-making and methods to achieve this
- the importance of analysing problems from a variety of perspectives
- the importance of identifying and prioritising the outcomes desired by all major stakeholders in considering project problems
- the importance of developing a range of possible options in solving problems
- the importance of involving a range of relevant people in generating possible solutions and how to do so

Communication
- how to present possible solutions in a way which helps relevant people to reach an informed and realistic judgement.

Planning
- the importance of drawing on personal experience and the relevant good practice of others and how to do so

Resource management
- how to make efficient and effective use of the resources available to the project.

Evidence requirements

You must prove that you *develop solutions to project problems* to the National Standard of competence.

To do this, you must provide evidence to convince your assessor that you consistently meet **all** the performance criteria.

Your evidence must be the result of real work activities undertaken by yourself. Evidence from simulated activities is **not** acceptable for this element.

You must show evidence that you solve at least **three** of the following types of **problems**
- technical
- financial
- resource-based
- project performance
- quality
- regulatory.

You must also show evidence that you solve problems for at least **two** of the following types of **projects**
- with strategic implications for the sponsor
- with substantial financial implications for the sponsor
- with a high level of complexity
- involving external organisations.

You must show evidence that you work with at least **two** of the following types of **team members**
- people exclusively involved in the project
- people who have other responsibilities and accountabilities
- people from outside your organisation.

You must, however, convince your assessor that you have the necessary knowledge, understanding and skills to be able to perform competently in respect of **all** types of **problems**, **projects** and **team members** listed above.

Manage the running of projects

Element G5.4

Maintain communication with project stakeholders

Performance criteria

You must ensure that

a) the key **stakeholders** receive timely, forward-looking and relevant information which is consistent with the **project** plans and helpful to the **project** achieving its goals

b) **team members** and sponsors have opportunities to contribute effectively to the information provided

c) the content of the information meets your **stakeholders'** needs, whilst maintaining agreements on confidentiality

d) the information is presented in styles and formats most appropriate to the types of **stakeholders** involved

e) the distribution methods are effective in reaching the key **stakeholders**

f) you actively seek and assess information from **stakeholders** which may affect the running of the **project**.

Knowledge requirements

You need to know and understand

Communication
- the methods which may be used to keep stakeholders up-to-date and how to select methods appropriate to different groups
- how to select content, styles, formats and distribution methods for different audiences and the importance of doing so

Information handling
- the importance of presenting information in a way which is consistent with agreements on confidentiality

Involvement and motivation
- the importance of involving other relevant people in producing information
- what contributions other relevant people can make to information and how to involve them

Organisational context
- the range of stakeholders you need to keep informed

Working relationships
- the importance of keeping all key stakeholders informed on project progress.

Evidence requirements

You must prove that you *maintain communication with project stakeholders* to the National Standard of competence.

To do this, you must provide evidence to convince your assessor that you consistently meet **all** the performance criteria.

Your evidence must be the result of real work activities undertaken by yourself. Evidence from simulated activities is **not** acceptable for this element.

You must show evidence that you maintain communication with **both** of the following types of **stakeholders**
- internal
- external.

You must also show evidence that you provide information for at least **two** of the following types of **projects**
- with strategic implications for the sponsor
- with substantial financial implications for the sponsor
- with a high level of complexity
- involving external organisations.

You must show evidence that you involve **two** of the following types of **team members**
- people exclusively involved in the project
- people who have other responsibilities and accountabilities
- people from outside your organisation.

You must, however, convince your assessor that you have the necessary knowledge, understanding and skills to be able to perform competently in respect of **all** types of **projects** and **team members** listed above.

Complete projects

Unit summary

This unit is about completing substantial, complex projects which are critical to the strategic objectives of the sponsoring organisation. The project sponsor may be internal or external to your organisation.

This unit contains two elements

G6.1 *Ensure the completion of project activities*
G6.2 *Evaluate the effectiveness of project planning and implementation.*

Personal competencies

In performing effectively in this unit, you will show that you

Acting assertively

- take a leading role in initiating action and making decisions
- take personal responsibility for making things happen
- take control of situations and events
- act in an assured and unhesitating manner when faced with a challenge
- say no to unreasonable requests
- state your own position and views clearly in conflict situations
- maintain your beliefs, commitment and effort in spite of set-backs or opposition

Communicating

- listen actively, ask questions, clarify points and rephrase others' statements to check mutual understanding
- adopt communication styles appropriate to listeners and situations, including selecting an appropriate time and place
- present difficult ideas and problems in ways that promote understanding

Focusing on results

- maintain a focus on objectives
- tackle problems and take advantage of opportunities as they arise
- focus personal attention on specific details that are critical to the success of a key event
- actively seek to do things better
- use change as an opportunity for improvement
- establish and communicate high expectations of performance, including setting an example to others
- monitor quality of work and progress against plans
- continually strive to identify and minimise barriers to excellence.

Complete projects

Element G6.1

Ensure the completion of project activities

Performance criteria

You must ensure that

a) the **project's** goals have been achieved to the agreed schedule, costs and quality criteria

b) all deliverables are handed over according to agreed procedures

c) you resolve any handover problems in a way which maintains an effective working relationship with the sponsor

d) you obtain agreement from the sponsor that all specified **project** work has been achieved

e) you collect information from the sponsor on the effectiveness of the **project** and their level of satisfaction with it

f) you confirm the completion of the **project** with **team members** and promptly authorise all associated work to be closed in a way which is consistent with your **project** plans

g) you authorise all the necessary procedures relating to finance, resources and personnel to be completed in accordance with organisational requirements

h) all records and documents relating to the **project** are accurate, complete and securely stored for future use.

Knowledge requirements

You need to know and understand

Customer relations

- common difficulties which may occur at the point of handover and how to address these
- how to maintain an effective working relationship with the sponsor at the point of project closure
- the importance of obtaining the sponsor's agreement that all specified work has been carried out

Monitoring and evaluation

- methods of ensuring that the agreed deliverables have been achieved
- the importance of storing records and documents for future use

Organisational context

- procedures for finance, resources and personnel which need to be followed at project closure
- the records and documents which need to be completed

Planning

- the plans for project closure
- the handover procedures for the project.

Evidence requirements

You must prove that you *ensure the completion of project activities* to the National Standard of competence.

To do this, you must provide evidence to convince your assessor that you consistently meet **all** the performance criteria.

Your evidence must be the result of real work activities undertaken by yourself. Evidence from simulated activities is **only** acceptable for performance criterion c).

You must show evidence that you complete the work of at least **two** of the following types of **projects**
- with strategic implications for the sponsor
- with substantial resource implications for the sponsor
- with a high level of complexity
- involving external organisations.

You must also show evidence that you work with at least **two** of the following types of **team members**
- people exclusively involved in the project
- people who have other responsibilities and accountabilities
- people from outside your organisation.

You must, however, convince your assessor that you have the necessary knowledge, understanding and skills to be able to perform competently in respect of **all** types of **projects** and **team members** listed above.

Complete projects

Element G6.2

Evaluate the effectiveness of project planning and implementation

Performance criteria

You must ensure that

a) you collect, verify and collate all key information relating to the planning and implementation of the **project** in ways which will assist effective **evaluation**

b) you include information which covers the perspectives of all key stakeholders

c) you accurately compare what was planned, what actually happened and what changes had to be made to the **project's** plans, scope and definition

d) you correctly identify reasons for variations to plans and the key lessons to be drawn from the **project**

e) you consult with **team members** and the sponsor on your **evaluation** and provide them with effective opportunities to contribute

f) you record and store your **evaluation** in a way which can be used to inform future **projects**

g) within the constraints of any agreements on confidentiality, you disseminate the results of your **evaluation** to **team members** and acknowledge the inputs which they made to the success of the **project**.

Knowledge requirements

You need to know and understand

Involvement and motivation

- the importance of involving other relevant people in the evaluation and methods to ensure their contributions are effective
- how to acknowledge the inputs of others in a way which rewards their contributions

Monitoring and evaluation

- the principles underpinning the monitoring and evaluation of projects and your role and responsibilities in relation to this
- how to identify, collect, verify and collate key information which will assist the evaluation
- how to identify the reasons for changes in project plans and implementation

Training and development

- how to identify the key lessons from an evaluation and why it is important to record and store evaluation results for future use
- the importance of communicating the results of your evaluation to relevant people and effective methods of doing so.

Evidence requirements

You must prove that you *evaluate the effectiveness of project planning and implementation* to the National Standard of competence.

To do this, you must provide evidence to convince your assessor that you consistently meet **all** the performance criteria.

Your evidence must be the result of real work activities undertaken by yourself. Evidence from simulated activities is **not** acceptable for this element.

You must show evidence that you evaluate at least **two** of the following types of **projects**

- with strategic implications for the sponsor
- with substantial resource implications for the sponsor
- with a high level of complexity
- involving external organisations.

You must also show evidence that you use **both** of the following types of **evaluation**

- quantitative
- qualitative

You must also show evidence that you involve **two** of the following types of **team members**

- people exclusively involved in the project
- people who have other responsibilities and accountabilities
- people from outside your organisation.

You must, however, convince your assessor that you have the necessary knowledge, understanding and skills to be able to perform competently in respect of **all** types of **projects** and **team members** listed above.

Notes
1. Page references for major topics of units are in **bold**
2. The sub-entry *teams* should be taken throughout to indicate *teams and individuals*

A

achievements, energy efficiency 142–3
acting assertively
    meetings 117
    own performance 43
    personnel 71, 109
    project 181, 191
    resource use 37
    teams 77, 91, 101
acting strategically
    energy efficiency 133, 139
    financial resources 63
    information for critical decisions 51
    information management/communication
        systems 123
    personnel 109
    project planning 173
    quality 145, 151
advantages/benefits
    change 20–1
    energy efficiency 140, 141
    quality **144–9**
advice for critical decisions 58–9
agreements and contracts 8–9, 125, 127
allocation
    financial resources 64–5
    work 92–3
analysis
    activity change 20, 21
    information for decision making 54–5
analytical techniques
    activity change 21, 23, 29
    customer requirements 13
    information 53, 55, 57, 125
    project 175, 185, 187
    quality 147, 149, 153, 155, 167
    resource use 31, 33
approved centre 3
assertive action *see* acting assertively
assessment of performance
    own 38, 39
    teams 86–7, 96–7

see also monitoring
assessor 3
assurance, quality **156–63**
audit
    energy efficiency 134–5
    quality compliance 166–7, 168–9

B

behaving ethically 43, 71, 101, 109
benefits *see* advantages
budgets for programmes of work 32–3, 34–5
building teams
    customer requirements 7
    meetings 117
    performance 77, 91, 101
    personnel 109
    quality compliance 165
    relationships, productive 43

C

chairing meetings 118–19
change management **16–27**, 185
colleagues and team members
    activity change 19, 21, 23, 25, 27
    customer requirements 11, 13, 15
    energy efficiency 135, 141
    financial resources 69
    information for critical decisions 57
    information/communication systems 125,
        127, 129
    own performance 39, 41
    personnel 73, 111, 113, 115
    project 77
        completion 192, 193, 194, 195
        running 182, 183, 184, 185, 186, 187, 188,
            189
    quality
        assurance 159, 161, 163
        compliance 167, 169, 171
        improvement 153, 155
    resource use 31, 33
    team performance 81, 85, 93, 94, 95, 102–3
    trust and support of 44–5
    see also relationships
communicating *see* personal competencies
communication
    activity change 17, 19, 21, 23, 25, 27
    customer requirements 7, 9, 11, 13, 15

energy efficiency 133, 135, 137, 139, 141, 143
financial resources 63, 67
information for critical decisions 51, 55, 57, 59
information management/communication
  systems 123, 129
meetings 117, 119, 121
own performance 37, 39
personnel 71, 73, 75, 109, 111, 115
project 173, 179, 181, 187, 188–9, 191
quality
  assurance 157, 158, 159, 161, 163
  compliance 165, 167, 169, 171
  improvement 151, 155
  promotion 145, 147, 148, 149
relationships, productive 43, 45, 47, 49
resource use 29, 31, 33
systems **122–31**
teams, performance of 91, 93, 95, 97, 99
  development 77, 79, 81, 89
  poor 101, 103
competence, management 39
completion of project **190–5**
compliance with quality systems **164–71**
constraints
  information for critical decisions 58, 59
  own performance 40, 41
  project 174, 175, 176, 177
  teams 94, 95, 97
continuous improvement
  activity change 19
  customer requirements 9, 11
  information/communication systems 129, 131
  personnel selection 75
  quality **150–5**, 163
  teams 79, 89, 97, 99
  see also improvement
contracts 8–9, 125, 127
control, project 178–9
corrective action
  quality compliance 168, 169
  resource use 34, 35
critical decisions, information for **50–9**
customers/customer relations
  energy efficiency 143
  project 175, 193
  quality 148–9, 159, 163
  requirements **6–15**
  teams, performance of 93

D

decision making
  analysis on information for 54–5
  critical, information for **50–9**
  see also thinking
delegation 40, 41, 93, 179
development
  own knowledge and skills 38–9
  plans to achieve project's goal 176–7
  quality improvement 152–3
  teams **76–89**
  see also training and development
disadvantages of change 20–1
disciplinary and grievance procedures 104–5
dismissal of team members 106–7

E

effectiveness
  project 194–5
  resource use **28–35**
energy efficiency
  improvement **132–7**
  promotion **138–43**
enhancement of performance
  own **36–41**
  team development **76–89**
equal opportunities 111, 169
  teams 79, 81, 83, 85, 87
ethical behaviour 43, 71, 101, 109
evaluation see monitoring
evidence requirements 1
expenditure 30–1, 34–5, 66–7
external organisations, people from
  activity change 19, 21, 23, 25, 27
  customer requirements 11, 13, 15
  information/communication systems 125,
    127, 129
  own performance 41
  personnel 111, 113, 115
  resource use 31, 33
  teams, performance of 79

F

feedback on performance of teams 98–9
financial resources 30–5, **62–9**
focusing on results see results
  activity change 17

  customer requirements 7
  meetings 117
  own performance 37
  project 173, 181, 191
  quality 151, 157, 165
  resource use 29
  teams, poor performance of 101
form
  advice and information 58, 59
  feedback 98, 99
format, energy efficiency 136, 137, 141

G

goals *see* objectives
guidance on values at work 48–9

H

health and safety 12–13, 137

I

identification of requirements
  information/communication 124–5
  personnel 72–3
implementation
  activity change 22–3, 26–7
  discipline and grievance 104–5
  information/communication systems 128–9
  project effectiveness 194–5
  quality system 152–3, **156–63**, 168–9
improvement
  activities 18–19
  energy efficiency **132–7**, 136–7
  information/communication systems 130, 131
  performance of team 82–3
  quality assurance 162–3
  teams, performance of 88–9
  see also continuous improvement
indicators, performance 134, 135
individuals
  learning and development 84–5; *see also*
    teams; training
influencing others
  activity change 17
  customer requirements 7
  energy efficiency 133, 139, 141
  financial resources 63
  information for critical decisions 51

  information management/communication
    systems 123
  personnel selection 71
  project 173
  quality 145, 151, 155, 157
  resource use 29
information handling and management
  activity change 19, 21
  critical decisions **50–9**
  customer requirements 9
  energy efficiency 137, 143
  management/communication systems
    122–31
  own performance 41
  personnel 73, 74, 75, 111, 113
  project running 189
  quality
    assurance 161, 163
    improvement 152, 153
    promotion 146, 147, 149
  relationships, productive 45
  resource use 31, 33, 35
  teams, performance of 92, 93, 96, 97, 99
    development 79, 87, 89
    poor 103, 104, 105, 107
  see also searching for information
involvement and motivation
  activity change 19, 21, 23, 27
  customer requirements 11
  financial resources 69
  information/communication systems 129, 131
  meetings 117
  personnel 73, 111, 113, 115
  project 183, 189, 195
  quality 149, 159, 161, 163
  resource use 31, 3335
  teams, performance of 93, 95, 97, 99
    development 79, 81, 83, 87, 89
    poor 107

J

jobs 114, 115; *see also* personnel

K

key roles 1–2
knowledge requirements 1
  agreements and contracts 9, 125, 127,

analytical techniques 13, 19, 21, 23, 31, 33, 53, 55, 57, 125, 147, 149, 153, 155, 167, 175, 185, 187

budgets 33, 35

change management 23, 25, 27, 185

communication 9, 11, 13, 15, 19, 21, 23, 25, 27, 31, 33, 39, 45, 47, 49, 55, 57, 59, 67, 73, 75, 79, 81, 89, 93, 95, 97, 99, 103, 111, 113, 115, 119, 121, 129, 135, 137, 141, 143, 147, 149, 155, 159, 161, 163, 167, 169, 171, 179, 187, 189

continuous improvement 9, 11, 19, 75, 79, 89, 97, 99, 129, 131, 163

customer relations 9, 15, 159, 163, 175, 193

delegation 41, 93, 179

disciplinary and grievance procedures 105, 107

energy efficiency 135, 137, 141, 143

equal opportunities 79, 81, 83, 85, 87, 111, 169

health and safety 13, 137

information handling 9, 19, 21, 31, 33, 35, 41, 45, 53, 55, 59, 73, 75, 79, 87, 89, 97, 99, 103, 105, 107, 111, 113, 125, 127, 137, 143, 149, 153, 161, 163, 189

involvement and motivation 11, 19, 21, 23, 27, 31, 33, 35, 69, 73, 79, 81, 83, 87, 89, 93, 95, 97, 99, 107, 111, 113, 115, 129, 131, 141, 155, 159, 161, 163, 183, 189, 195

leadership styles 83, 119,183

legal requirements 65, 69, 73, 75, 105, 107, 111, 125, 127, 135

management competence 39

meetings 119, 121

monitoring and evaluation 15, 19, 27, 41, 65, 67, 85, 103, 113, 131, 135, 153, 155, 169, 171, 193, 195

organisational context 9, 11, 13, 15, 19, 21, 23, 25, 27, 31, 35, 39, 45, 47, 49, 53, 57, 59, 65, 67, 69, 73, 75, 79, 81, 87, 89, 93, 95, 97, 105, 107, 119, 125, 135, 137, 141, 143, 147, 149, 153, 155, 167, 169, 171, 175, 179, 189, 193

planning 11, 21, 23, 27, 41, 81, 95, 111, 127, 129, 131, 175, 177, 187, 193

project management 185

providing support 45, 67, 85, 97, 103, 113, 115, 183

quality management 15, 147, 149, 155, 159, 161, 167, 169, 171

recruitment and selection 73, 75, 179

redeployment and redundancy 111, 115

resource management 31, 65, 67, 69, 125, 127, 129, 153, 155, 179, 185, 187

strategic planning 147

team working 169

time management 41

training and development 39, 79, 81, 83, 87, 179, 195

working relationships 45, 47, 49, 67, 103, 105, 107, 113, 121, 163, 177, 185, 189

workplace organisation 13

L

leadership/leadership styles 83, 119, 182–3

learning, individual 84–5; *see also* training and development

legal requirements
  customers 8
  energy efficiency 135
  financial resources 65, 69
  information/communication systems 125, 127
  personnel selection 73, 75
  teams, performance of 105, 107

M

maintenance of quality assurance 160–1

management competence 39

managers and sponsors, higher-level
  activity change 19, 21, 23, 25, 27
  customer requirements 11, 13, 15
  energy efficiency 135, 141
  financial resources 69
  information for critical decisions 57
  information management/communication systems 125, 127, 129
  own performance 39
  personnel 73, 111, 113, 115
  quality
    assurance 159, 161, 163
    compliance 167, 169, 171
    improvement 153, 155
  relationships, productive 49
  resource use 31, 33
  teams, performance of 81, 93
  trust and support of 46–7

managing self **36–41**, 43, 109

mandatory units 5–59

meetings **116–21**

poor performance of teams **100–7**
preparation for personnel redeployment 112–13
problems 102–3, 186–7
productive relationships, enhancing 2, **36–41**
productive working environment 12–13
project management
    completion **190–5**
    planning **172–9**, 184–5, 194–5
    running **180–9**
promotion
    energy efficiency **138–43**
    quality **144–9**, 154–5
proposals, expenditure 66–7
providing support
    colleagues and team members 44–5
        financial resources 67
    individual learning 84–5
    managers and sponsors 46–7
    personnel redeployment/redundancies
        112–13, 115
    project planning 183
    relationships, productive 45
    teams, performance of 85, 97, 102–3
purpose
    meeting 118, 119
    team assessment 86, 87, 96, 97

Q

quality management 2, 15
    assurance implementation **156–63**
    compliance with systems **164–71**
    continuous improvement **150–5**
    promotion **144–9**

R

reasons for dismissal 106, 107
recipients of advice/information 58, 59
recommendations on improvement of quality
    assurance 162–3
recruitment and selection **70–5**, 179
redeployment of personnel 110–11, 112–13
redundancy 114–15
relationships *see* working relationships
reporting 46–7, 170–1
requirements
    information and communication 124–5
    organisational, customer requirements and 8,
        9, 14, 15

    personnel 72–3
    see also knowledge and evidence; legal *and*
       under customers
resources/resource management
    effective use of **28–35**
    information/communication systems 125,
       127, 129
    optimisation of own 40–1
    project 178–9, 184–5, 187
    quality improvement 153, 155
    see also energy efficiency; financial resources
results *see* focusing on results

S

safety 12–13, 137
searching for information
    activity change 17
    critical decisions 51
    energy efficiency 133, 139
    financial resources 63
    management and communication systems 123
    meetings 117
    personnel 71
    quality 145, 151, 165
    resource use 29
Scottish Vocational Qualification (SVQ) 1, 3
self-management **36–41**, 43, 109
situation of feedback 98, 99
skills, own, development of 38–9
sources of information 52, 53
specialists
    activity change 19, 21, 23, 25, 27
    customer requirements 15
    energy efficiency 135, 141
    information for critical decisions 57
    information management/communication
       systems 125, 127, 129
    own performance 39
    personnel 73, 111, 113, 115
    project 177
    quality
       assurance 159, 161, 163
       compliance 167, 169, 171
       improvement 153, 155
    relationships, productive 49
    resource use 31, 33
    teams, performance of 79, 81
specifications, personnel 72, 73

methods of obtaining information 52, 53
monitoring and evaluation
  activity change 19, 20–1, 26, 27
  customer requirements 15
  energy efficiency 135
  expenditure proposals 66–7
  financial resources 65, 67
  information/communication systems 130–1
  own performance 41
  personnel 113
  project 184–5, 193, 194–5
  quality 152–3, 155, 160, 161, 169, 171
  resource use 34
  teams 85, 96, 97, 103
  see also assessment
motivation see involvement

N

National Vocational Qualification (NVQ) 1, 3
needs development of teams 78–9
negotiations and activity change 24, 25

O

objectives
  optimisation of own resources 40–1
  project, achieving 176–7
  of work to teams 94–5
obstacles to change 22, 23
opportunities
  activity improvement 18–19
  quality promotion 148, 149
optimisation of own resources 40–1
optional units 61–195
organisational context
  activity change **16–27**
  customer requirements 8, 9, 11, 13, 14, 15
  energy efficiency 135, 137, 141, 143
  financial resources 65, 67, 69
  information for critical decisions 53, 57, 59
  information management/communication
    systems 125
  meetings 119
  own performance 39
  personnel selection 73, 75
  project 175, 179, 189, 193
  quality 147, 149, 153, 155, 167, 169, 171
  relationships, productive 45, 47, 49
  resource use 31, 35

teams, performance of 93, 95, 97
  development 79, 81, 87, 89
  poor 105, 107
  see also constraints
own performance see self-management

P

participation in meetings 120–1
performance
  energy efficiency 134–5
  improvement and team development 82–3
  indicators 134, 135
  own see self–management
  quality improvement 152–3
  see also enhancement; team working
personal competencies 1
  acting assertively 37, 43, 51, 71, 77, 91, 101,
    109, 117, 181, 191
  acting strategically 63, 109, 123, 133, 139,
    145, 151, 173
  behaving ethically 43, 71, 101, 109
  building teams 7, 43, 77, 91, 101, 109, 117, 165
  communicating 7, 17, 29, 37, 43, 51, 63, 71,
    77, 91, 101, 109, 117, 123, 133, 139, 145,
    151, 157, 165, 173, 181, 191
  focusing on results 7, 17, 29, 37, 101, 117,
    151, 157, 165, 173, 181, 191
  influencing others 7, 17, 29, 51, 63, 71, 117,
    123, 133, 139, 145, 151, 157, 173
  managing self 37, 43, 109
  searching for information 29, 51, 63, 71, 117,
    133, 139, 145, 151, 165
  thinking and taking decisions 7, 29, 37, 43, 51,
    63, 71, 77, 91, 117, 123, 145, 151,157, 165,
    173, 181
personnel management
  redeployment and redundancies **108–15**
  selection **70–5**, 179
planning
  activity change 21, 22–3
  audit of compliance with quality systems 166–7
  customer requirements 10–11
  information/communication systems 127,
    129, 131
  personnel 110–11
  project **172–9**, 184–5, 187, 193, 194–5
  resource use 41
  team performance (work plans) 80–1, 94–5

stakeholders/sponsors, project
   communication with 188–9
   planning 174–5, 182, 183
strategic action *see* acting strategically
strategic planning and quality 147
suppliers
   energy 141, 143
   quality 148–9
   teams, performance of 93
support *see* providing support

T

team working **90–9**
   development **76–89**
   poor **100–7**
   project 182–3
   quality compliance 185
   see also colleagues and team members
thinking and taking decisions
   activity change 17
   customer requirements 7
   financial resources 63
   information for critical decisions 51
   information management/communication
     systems 123
   meetings 117
   own performance 37
   personnel selection 71
   project 173, 181
   quality 145, 151, 157, 165
   relationships, productive 43
   resource use 29
   teams, performance of 77, 91
time management 41
training and development
   project 179, 195
   resource use 39
   teams 79, 81, 83, 84–5, 87
   see also development
trends and developments
   information/communication systems 130, 131
   quality 154, 155
trust 44–5, 46–7

U

units of competence 1

users (and others) of information/
  communication systems 124, 125, 126, 127,
  128, 129, 130, 131

V

values at work, guidance on 48–9

W

work environment 12–13, 137
working relationships
   enhancing productive **36–41**
   financial resources 67
   meetings 121
   personnel 113
   project 177, 185, 189
   quality assurance 163
   teams 103, 105, 107
workplace organisation 13